Ever Since Sinai

Ever Since Sinai

A MODERN VIEW OF TORAH

Revised Third Edition

JAKOB J. PETUCHOWSKI

B. ARBIT BOOKS
PUBLISHERS • BOOKSELLERS • DISTRIBUTORS

THIRD EDITION 1979

ISBN: 0-930038-11-8
LC Number: 79-64324
Printed in the United States of America

B. Arbit Books
8050 N. Port Washington Road
Milwaukee, Wisconsin 53217

To ELIZABETH

Proverbs 31:26

Acknowledgments

THE author wishes to thank the following publishers for graciously permitting him to quote from works published by them:

Oxford University Press (quotation from Theodore H. Robinson, *A History of Israel.* 1932); Macmillan and Company Limited (quotations from Leo Baeck, *The Essence of Judaism.* 1936); The Jewish Publication Society of America (quotation from Leo Baeck, *Judaism and Christianity.* 1958); The Sheldon Press (quotation from Edward Robertson, "Law and Religion Amongst the Samaritans," in *Judaism and Christianity,* Vol. III, ed. E. I. J. Rosenthal. 1938); and Alfred A. Knopf Inc. (quotation from Sigmund Freud, *Moses and Monotheism.* Vintage Books, 1955).

Some of the material in Chapters Three, Six and Seven of this book has previously appeared in articles written by the author for *Judaism, Commentary,* and *Jewish Frontier,* respectively. It is used here in a somewhat altered form with the kind permission of the Editors concerned.

J. J. P.

Table of Contents

Preface to the Third Edition

Ever Since Sinai, which, since its first appearance in 1961, has been used in many college and university courses as well as in adult education classes and high school departments of religious schools, wants to fulfil a twofold task. In the first place, it tries to convey a sense of what Torah has meant to past Jewish generations, what it means to some modern Jews, and what it could conceivably mean to others. It does not deal with the concept of Torah in isolation from related theological concepts, which would be a caricature, but within the framework of a whole complex of beliefs such as the doctrines of God, Election, Revelation, and the old Rabbinic conviction that an Oral Torah accompanies and supplements the Written Torah. From this perspective, *Ever Since Sinai* might be called a "phenomenology of Torah."

Yet there is also a second aim which the author regards as being of no less importance. A considerable proportion of today's American Jewry is university educated. A university education, particularly in the Humanities, involves the exposure of the student to the kind of critical method with which various bodies of literature are studied. Torah, among other things, is also a body of literature. If, then, Torah literature is approached in a scholarly and critical frame of mind, many a cherished belief of the past will be seen to rest on foundations which modern scholarship calls into question. This situation has led, on the one hand, to a dogmatic rejection of the methods and conclusions of modern biblical scholarship, and, on the other, to an equally dogmatic rejection of religious belief. It is, however, the contention of this author that there is yet a third possibility. Neither scholarship nor belief have to be rejected—if it can only be established in what realms scholarship is, and in what areas it is not competent to render its verdicts, and if it can be shown that the essential religious beliefs concerning Torah are not invariably bound up with those putative historical data which are now doubted by critical and objective scholarship. This, *Ever Since Sinai* attempts to do.

Many Jews who are affiliated with either the Reform or the Conservative wings of Judaism (and possibly even some who are only nominally Orthodox) not only have a basic commitment to the Jewish religious heritage, but they are also searching for an appreciation of that heritage which does not reject modern scholarship or neglect the predicaments of modern life. In order to meet the needs of such Jews, the seventh chapter of *Ever Since Sinai* has been enlarged in this third edition by the inclusion of some considerations which may help to lead the reader from a mere theory of Torah to the deeds and to the way of life in which Torah finds concrete expression.

Readers and reviewers of previous editions of this book have encountered difficulties in their attempts to pigeonhole the author in one of the ready-made "denominational" categories of American Judaism— Orthodox, Conservative, and Reform. It is good that this should have been so, and we trust that the present edition contains nothing which would make that pigeonholing any easier. For the labels of yesteryear are rapidly losing such vestiges of significance as they may still possess. To some extent, those labels do indeed serve as quantitative indicators of the degree of traditional Jewish observance. But the real division in American Judaism today, cutting across the conventional "denominational" lines, is the division between those who, in one way or another, see God involved in the process of Torah development, and those who see Torah as a purely human document. In terms of that divison, the author of this book sides with the former.

Ever Since Sinai does not claim to answer all the important questions to which the subject of Torah gives rise in the modern age. The book has a far more modest aim. The author will consider himself amply rewarded if the book will serve as a guidepost to the directions in which, with further effort, answers to some important questions may be found, and new questions will be raised.

Cincinnati, Ohio
Hanukkah 5739 (1978)

Jakob J. Petuchowski

CHAPTER ONE

Looking at
a Marriage Contract

THE visitor at a Jewish museum can spend hours in the contemplation of illuminated Hebrew marriage contracts,—the most beautiful among them coming from 17th and 18th century Italy. The artist can study the colors, the drawings, and the illuminations. The historian may muse on the dates, the names, and the places. The student of Jewish Law will check on the accuracy of the terminology. It is really wonderful to see how much relevant and important material there is extant in what, after all, is nothing but a dry-as-dust legal document, in which a Jewish husband promises to abide by the regulations which Jewish Law, in its Talmudic formulation, has laid down as governing a marriage entered into "according to the law of Moses and Israel."

Suppose, then, that our visitor's attention is arrested

by a particularly colorful specimen of this type of marriage contract. Two stately columns, a bold arch, and a pleasing assortment of flowers and birds surround the traditional text. And the text itself informs him that on a Monday, the twenty-fourth day of the spring month of Nisan, 1723, in the city of Ancona, a certain young man, Menahem the son of Abraham, said to the maiden, Flavia the daughter of Ishmael, "be thou my wife according to the law of Moses and Israel." And Menahem then proceeds to outline all the obligations he has taken upon himself. And the whole document is duly signed by witnesses.

No doubt, we suspect that prior to the execution of this document there has been some romance between Menahem and Flavia. But what was there really between them? How did they feel about each other? What, indeed, was it that made them decide to enter that union to which this marriage contract testifies? Now, there is much which this marriage contract can tell the artist and the historian, but the answers to these questions cannot be obtained from it. There is no space in a legal and official document of this sort for the expression of personal feelings. They, at best, will have to be presupposed by the historian, but they are not, strictly speaking, his province. Unless, of course, he should be fortunate enough to chance upon a *cache* of Italian-Jewish correspondence of the early 18th century, containing the letters which Menahem and Flavia wrote to each other before and throughout their married life. A find like that would really bring to life the legal terminology of our marriage contract.

But this is not a book about Jewish art, or about the history of the Jews in Italy. This is a book about the meaning of *Torah*, and the story of the Italian Jewish marriage contract merely served us as an introduction. It is, we hope, an introduction which is not quite as far-fetched as at first sight might appear. It is, we believe, directly relevant.

From the writings of the Hebrew Prophets through those of the later Rabbis and mystics there emerges the favorite metaphor to describe the relationship of God and Israel, to wit: that of a *marriage*. God, says Jeremiah, remembers Israel's "love as a bride" (Jeremiah 2:2). Hosea likens Israel's backsliding from God to the unfaithfulness of his own wife; but he also looks forward to the time of reconciliation, when God will say to His people: "And I will betroth thee unto Me for ever." (Hosea 2:21.) The Song of Songs is almost unanimously understood by the commentators of the Synagogue as an allegory describing the courtship of God and Israel, climaxing in the "marriage ceremony" at Mount Sinai. It is, therefore, not strange that, continuing the same line of thought, there should be rabbinic references to the Torah in terms of the "marriage contract" legalizing that "union." [1]

The metaphor of the "marriage contract" used by the Rabbis of old to describe the Torah has a usefulness for the modern Jew which the early writers could hardly have envisaged. For, like the Italian marriage contract we have mentioned, it suggests to us the areas of competence in which the various modern disciplines of literary and historical criticism have their

3

being. It also suggests to us the particular realm in which we can obtain enlightenment only if and when other material becomes available to us which is comparable to the "love letters" in which the partners to this union express their true feelings about the state of "matrimony" to which the "contract" testifies.

We begin, then, by taking note of such knowledge and information as is accessible to him who, with complete scientific objectivity, approaches the document in question. After that, we shall look for any "love letters" which might possibly have survived, and then try to make sense of the document in terms of that deeper insight.

Etymology

There is, of course, first of all, the word *torah* itself. It is used in so many different contexts that, before speaking about *the* Torah, we had better look a little at its history. In the Hebrew Bible there are passages where the word *torah* clearly has the sense of "instruction," the sort of guidance parents give to their children. For example, the Book of Proverbs (1:8) says:

"Hear, my son, the instruction of thy father,
And forsake not the *torah* of thy mother."

The same book (31:26) mentions about the "woman of valor" that

"She openeth her mouth with wisdom;
And the *torah* of kindness is on her tongue."

4

Just as *torah* denotes the "instruction" given by parents to their children, so does it denote, in other parts of the Bible, the "instruction" which God gives to the children of men. In this sense Eliphaz the Temanite advises his friend Job:

> "Receive, I pray thee, *torah* from His mouth,
> And lay up His words in thy heart."
>
> (Job 22:22.)

So far, none of the uses of *torah* we have considered has had any specific bearing on law-giving and legal systems. Yet it is in the latter sense that the word frequently occurs throughout the Bible. "This is the *torah* of the burnt-offering," we read in Leviticus 6:2, and this introduction is followed by an enumeration of all the steps involved in that particular sacrificial act. The procedure involved in the ritual cleansing of the leper is introduced by the words: "This shall be the *torah* of the leper in the day of his cleansing." (Leviticus 14:2.)

Torah is also the specific legal guidance given by the priest to him who comes to the sanctuary to enquire after a verdict not provided by the existing codes of law. Once the priests have rendered such a verdict, the Israelite is admonished: "According to the *torah* which they shall teach thee, and according to the judgment which they shall tell thee, thou shalt do; thou shalt not turn aside from the sentence which they shall declare unto thee, to the right hand, nor to the left." (Deuteronomy 17:11.) Here, then, *torah* seems to be used in the sense of "judgment" and "sentence."

But not only the individual law or decision is called *torah*. We also find the word applied to whole collections of ordinances and cultic as well as moral provisions. When we read in Deuteronomy 1:5 that "beyond the Jordan, in the land of Moab, Moses undertook to expound this *torah*," the reference is clearly to the Book of Deuteronomy of which this is one of the opening verses. This same book of the Bible seems to be referred to in II Kings, chapter 22, where we read about a book being found in the days of King Josiah. And it was when this king "had heard the words of the book of the *torah*, that he rent his clothes." (verse 11.)

In the course of time, the word *torah* was applied to the final redaction of all the legal codes and narrative portions which go into the making of the Five Books traditionally ascribed to Moses. *Torah* denoting the Pentateuch is a term which has been retained in Jewish usage. We speak of "reading the Torah" when we refer to that reading from the Scriptures which is taken from the Five Books of Moses. But this is *torah* only in its *narrowest sense*. Whatever definition of *torah* we are inclined to accept, one thing is certain: that, when the Jews called the Pentateuch *torah*, they did so because they accepted it as guidance from God. But this guidance did not cease with the demise of Moses. There were the Prophets, and there were the singers and the sages. They, too, were believed to have contributed their share to the Scriptures under the guidance of divine inspiration,—even though it was held that the degree of their inspiration was lower than that of Moses. And so we find that the word *torah* is used to describe the Bible as a whole, that is: The Five Books of Moses (i.e., *torah* in its narrowest sense) as well as the Prophets and the Writings.

Now, it was a claim of Pharisaic Judaism—a claim we shall have to discuss later in some greater detail—that God revealed to Moses not only a Written Torah, but an *Oral* Torah as well. The contents of this Oral Torah, or at least a part of them, later found their way into the literary productions of Rabbinic Judaism, into the Mishnah and into the Gemara. The result was that *torah,* in a wider sense, could now be used to describe *post-biblical* literature in addition to the Bible. Yet the history of our word did not stop there, either. Jewish life is a God-centered life. There are no areas in it for which religion does not provide. Everything is understood in terms of *torah.* It was thus natural for later teachers to claim that "the mere custom of our fathers is *torah!*" [2] But once we have reached this stage in the use of our word, it is legitimate to say that *torah* can be, and has been, used as a synonym for the *totality of Judaism.* This would be *torah* in its widest sense.

We have, however, not yet dealt with the question why *torah,* in any of its various meanings, should have been called *torah* in the first place. What, in other words, is the etymology of this word? Here, as in so many other matters connected with *torah,* there is no unanimity among scholars. One thing, though, is clear: the noun *torah* is derived from a verbal root *YaRaH;* and it is here that the difficulty sets in.

YaRaH means to throw, or to shoot. We know that

the priests of many ancient peoples, in determining the oracles of their gods, used some kind of sacred dice. A "yes" would be shown in one way, a "no" in another. And this "yes" or "no" would be understood as the answer of the god to any question presented to him by the priests. Of course, the questions had to be formulated in such a way that a "yes or no" answer could be deemed adequate. It is very likely that a similar procedure was followed in ancient Israel. The *urim* and *thummim,* mentioned in connection with the high-priest's breastplate (Exodus 28:30), seem to have had just such a function.

When Saul wanted to know on a particular occasion why Israel had suffered defeat at the hands of the Philistines, he consulted the *urim* and *thummim.* In I Samuel 14:41 (corrected here in the light of the Septuagint reading, the Greek version of the Bible), we read the following characteristic statement: "And Saul said: Lord, God of Israel, why hast Thou not answered Thy servant this day? If this iniquity be in me or in Jonathan my son, Lord, God of Israel, give *urim;* but if it be in Thy people Israel, give *thummim.* Then Jonathan and Saul were taken by lot; and the people escaped."

It is the use of oracles of this kind which suggests to some scholars that the early Israelite priests were in the habit of *throwing (YaRaH)* sacred dice to obtain God's answers to their questions. Once the answer had been obtained in this fashion, the priests handed it down as *torah. Torah,* therefore, even long after the

8

oracular use of *urim* and *thummim* had been discarded, would denote a priestly teaching of a moral or a ceremonial nature which was attributed to a divine source.

Seeing that *YaRaH* does mean to throw, there is something suggestive about this theory. But not all scholars agree with it. For one thing, in a number of related languages *YaRaH* does not mean to throw, or to shoot, but rather: to teach, to give information, to lead, and to guide. For another, in Hebrew itself, in one of the conjugations of the verbal root *YaRaH* the word means to show, to point out, to teach, and to direct. It is used, moreover, in contexts which have nothing whatever to do with priestly oracles. The view has, therefore, been expressed that there are actually two different roots *YaRaH* in the Hebrew language. One means to throw, and to shoot. The other means to guide, and to instruct. And the word *torah* is derived from the latter, and not from the former, word.

Yet interesting as these speculations are, it is not our purpose to establish scientific conclusions. In the long run, it is not really so important what a word *originally* meant, but *what it has come to mean,*—particularly in the sources with which we are concerned. But even here the meaning of *torah* remains somewhat ambiguous. When the Torah was translated into Greek, some time in the third century B.C.E., the Hebrew word *torah* was rendered by the Greek word *nomos*. And *nomos* means law! Here, at any rate, there were Jews who felt that the Torah was Law. It was on the basis of this Greek translation of the Bible that the Apostle

9

Paul described the Judaism of his time as being a system of "salvation by works," and as inducing the Jew to stand justified before God in terms of his legal obedience. From Paul the world has learned to look upon Judaism as a "legalistic" religion, contrasting it—unfavorably—with the religion of "faith" and of "love" said to be contained in the New Testament.

There is no doubt that in contemporary Palestinian Judaism, the Judaism of the Rabbis, there were those who, had they been compelled to translate the word *torah* into Greek, would likewise have chosen the word for "law." There were those, in other words, who saw the end-all and be-all of the Torah in its *legal* provisions. A Rabbi Isaac could raise the question why the Torah begins with the story of creation,—seeing that the first *law* addressed to the people of Israel does not occur before the twelfth chapter of the Book of Exodus.[3] Similarly, the teacher who felt that the Torah should have begun with the Ten Commandments, had it not been for the need of the Lawgiver to make Himself known to His subjects beforehand, must have been one of those who understood Torah primarily as law.[4]

But, by and large, the Palestinian sages leave us in no doubt that, though law was a very important part *of* Torah, the scope of Torah was wider by far. Torah, to them, was the instrument with which God created the world. It was the sum-total of all wisdom and knowledge. It was Teaching,—with a capital "T." They valued its narrative parts no less than its legal sections, and they clearly saw the finger of God in the historical events narrated in its pages.

Law or Teaching

The question whether Torah is primarily Law, or primarily Teaching, is a question which has been discussed through the millennia. It became very topical again at the beginning of the modern period. Jewish theologians in 19th-century Germany heatedly debated the issue whether Torah was *Gesetz* (Law) or *Lehre* (Teaching). The philosopher Moses Mendelssohn (1729/1786) had been indirectly responsible for starting that discussion. Mendelssohn, though in practice a fully observant Jew, was, philosophically, a Deist. He believed in the Religion of Reason, and felt that the "eternal verities" did not have to be revealed by God supernaturally. They were universally implanted in the human mind. And since the "eternal verities" were the possession of all of humankind, there was no need for a Hebrew Bible to promulgate them. Yet Mendelssohn was far from denying the Sinaitic Revelation. He firmly believed that such a revelation had taken place,—that God had, indeed, revealed the Torah to Israel. But the Torah, for Mendelssohn, was the peculiar *Law* which God had ordained for Israel, and which Israel was bound to observe,—at any rate, until such a time as God would see fit to revoke it again, as publicly and as spectacularly as He had originally revealed it.

The generations immediately succeeding Mendelssohn found that they could maintain the "eternal verities" just as well within the framework of other religious denominations. They had little use for a divine revelation of Torah concerning itself exclusively with just those legal and ceremonial provisions which interfered with the process of gaining a firm foothold in cultured European society. To remain a Jew merely for the sake of a "revealed legislation" was not worth the effort to them.

It was in opposition to Mendelssohn's narrowing down of the concept of Torah to that of "Law," and partly as an act of self-defense *vis-à-vis* the protagonists of an unbending Orthodoxy, that some of the early thinkers in Reform Judaism maintained rather vociferously that Torah was Teaching (*Lehre*) rather than Law. Disagreeing with Mendelssohn, they saw the purpose of Revelation in the imparting of religious truths. These were the essence of the Torah, and immutable. Law, on the other hand, so the Reformers claimed, always had to be in accordance with the needs of the times. As such, it was the changing element in religion. Its provisions could, under certain circumstances, become out-dated. Samuel Holdheim (1806/1860) spoke of the "essence of Judaism" which could be defined "without the necessity of activating this inward faith by means of external ceremonies." [5]

As with so many other "either/or" formulations, the answer here, too, is undoubtedly "both!" Taking just the few illustrations of the biblical use of the word *torah* which we have cited in this chapter, it should have been evident by now that in some instances the word can mean nothing but "law," while in others it means, with equal certainty, "teaching," "guidance,"

or "instruction,"—with no legalistic overtones what-
soever. The Torah, as a whole, can therefore legiti-
mately be described as the "Law *and* Lore of Judaism."
That one's own understanding of, or commitment to,
the "Law" may be different from that of earlier generations should be no reason for failing to do justice to a
phenomenon within its own setting.

Authorship of the Torah

We come now to the question of how the Torah
(in its narrow sense of denoting the Pentateuch) came
into being. This is a relatively modern question. For
over two millennia it had been held as a matter of
course that the Five Books of Moses were indeed what
they claimed to be: five books written by Moses. As we
shall have occasion to see, the assumed fact that these
books were written by Moses was not held to be nearly
as important as another basic assumption: that Moses
served as the vehicle of *God's* Revelation. The Divine,
rather than the Mosaic, authorship of the Pentateuch
was an item of Jewish dogmatics. But that God dictated
the Five Books to Moses, or that Moses wrote them under immediate divine inspiration, of that there had,
until comparatively recent times, been no doubt. There
was, of course, the matter of the burial of Moses described in the last chapter of Deuteronomy. Here one
had the choice of assuming that God dictated these
verses, while Moses wrote them down with a tear in his
eye, or of accepting the somewhat more rationalistic

view that Joshua wrote them down after the death of Moses.

This is not to say that some apparent contradictions within the text of the Torah have not been noted long ago. But there were ways and means of dealing with them. Take, for example, the law in Leviticus 18:16 and 20:21, which clearly forbids one's marriage to his sister-in-law. The very opposite seems to be implied in Deuteronomy 25:5, where a man is actually *commanded* to marry his sister-in-law after his brother's death. Yet the Rabbis of the Talmud had no difficulty in reconciling the two passages. The law in Leviticus, they said, applies to the case where the dead brother has left children, whereas the law in Deuteronomy states specifically that the marriage to one's brother's widow is mandatory only in the case where he has left no offspring.

Similarly, in Deuteronomy 16:22, the erection of a sacred pillar is expressly prohibited. It is stated there that "the Lord thy God hateth" the sacred pillar. Yet in Genesis 28:18 we are told that the Patriarch Jacob did, in fact, erect such a pillar at Beth-El; and there is not the slightest hint of criticism implied in this account. The Rabbis explained this apparent contradiction in terms of the changing circumstances of religious life. "The sacred pillar was beloved in the days of the Patriarchs; it was hateful in the days of their descendants."

Again, the clear statement, in Exodus 20:5, that God "visits the iniquity of the fathers upon the children" seems to be contradicted by Ezekiel 18:1-4, where the Prophet—*in the name of God*—emphatically rejects the view that the children are made to suffer for the sins of their fathers. The Rabbis tried to do justice to both positions by limiting the application of Exodus 20:5 to the case where "the children continue to do the wicked deeds of their fathers."

Even more striking is the contradiction between Exodus 13:6 and Deuteronomy 16:8. In the former verse we are told that, on the Feast of Unleavened Bread, we are to eat unleavened bread for seven days. In the latter verse we are told to eat unleavened bread for *six* days! But the Rabbis found a way of resolving this difficulty, too. They did so by adducing yet a third Scripture verse, Leviticus 23:14, in which the eating of new corn is permitted only after the bringing of the 'omer sacrifice; and the 'omer sacrifice takes place on the *second* day of Passover. In other words, Exodus 13:6 has reference to the eating of unleavened bread throughout the festival, while Deuteronomy 16:8 refers to the eating of such unleavened bread as has been made with *new* flour.

Such illustrations could be multiplied. Much of the dialectic of the Talmud is, in fact, applied to the harmonizing of apparently contradictory passages in the Scriptures. One of the thirteen principles by which the early Rabbis interpreted the Bible states: "When two texts contradict each other, the meaning can be determined only when a third text is found which harmonizes them."

Abraham Ibn Ezra

Rather unique is the 12th-century Spanish-Jewish commentator, Abraham Ibn Ezra, who seems to have had some doubts, not as to the Mosaic authorship of the Pentateuch as such, but as to the Mosaic authorship of certain specific passages within that Pentateuch. Thus Ibn Ezra was puzzled by the words, "and the Canaanite was then in the land," in Genesis 12:6. These words could surely have been written only by someone who lived when the Canaanite was *no longer* in the land! But that happened *after* the days of Moses to whom the words are attributed. Again, the statement in Deuteronomy 1:1 that "these are the words which Moses spoke unto all Israel beyond the Jordan," makes sense only if we assume that it was penned by someone living West of the Jordan. But Moses is said to have remained and died East of the Jordan. Ibn Ezra finds the words puzzling. There are a number of such passages in the Pentateuch which call forth Ibn Ezra's comment that a "secret" is involved. Yet he never spells out that secret, and it has even been claimed by modern Orthodox scholars that Ibn Ezra never intended to cast aspersions on the Mosaic authorship of such passages.

Still, Ibn Ezra's careful little hints were to have their repercussions in the literature of modern Philosophy. Baruch Spinoza (1632/1677) quotes Ibn Ezra at length in the eighth chapter of his *Theologico-Political Treatise*. Saying that Ibn Ezra, "a man of enlightened intelligence, and no small learning, . . . dared not express his meaning openly, but confined himself to dark hints," Spinoza proceeds to elucidate what, to him, was the purport of Ibn Ezra's comments. Spinoza, quoting Ibn Ezra as evidence, quite decidedly denies the Mosaic authorship of the Pentateuch, and suggests that the work might well be attributed to Ezra the Scribe (5th century B.C.E.). Some of the conclusions arrived at by Spinoza are remarkably close to those which were quite independently reached by more recent scholarship. In his own days, however, Spinoza's ingenious reconstructions of the literary history of the Bible seem to have had no further echoes in the world of biblical scholarship.

Modern Criticism

Modern biblical scholarship really begins with a French physician, Jean Astruc (1684/1766), who wrote a book on the different sources Moses must have used in constructing his account of the Creation. Astruc had noticed that different chapters in the Bible use different names of God. Thus, in Genesis 1, the Deity is referred to as *Elohim* (commonly translated as "God"), while in Genesis 2, He is called YHWH (commonly translated as "Lord").

Astruc, however, was not the first to notice this. The use of different divine names was well known to the Rabbis of old. And they had their own explanation for it. *Elohim,* in Hebrew, can also mean "judge," while the classic description of YHWH is given in Exodus 34:6, "The LORD, the LORD, God, merciful and gracious, long-suffering, and abundant in goodness and truth." The Rabbis reasoned, therefore, that whenever the name "God" occurs, it describes God in His "quality of justice," and whenever "the LORD" is used, it refers to God in His "quality of mercy." Applying this to the first two chapters of Genesis, they explained that, at first, God meant to create the world with the "quality of justice" alone. But, foreseeing that the world could not endure in this manner, He joined to it the "quality of mercy." [7]

The conclusions reached by Astruc were different. He discovered that the narratives using the different names of God were independent units. They make sense one without the other. Astruc, of course, merely assumed that Moses had acted as an editor in this instance. But the existence of different "sources" which went into the making of the Pentateuch was a hypothesis of far-reaching consequences. Later generations were no longer inhibited by the traditional belief that Moses wrote the Pentateuch, nor did they limit themselves to the assumption that there were only *two* "sources."

Expanded, modified, and refined by a number of scholars, the hypothesis about the existence of a number of "sources" out of which the Pentateuch was constructed reached its classical formulation in the works of the German scholar, Julius Wellhausen (1844/ 1918). By that time, there was nothing Mosaic left about the Pentateuch. Instead, it was regarded as a mosaic of different sources, and the task of biblical

scholarship was understood to be that of separating
out these various sources, and of tracing their historical
and religious backgrounds. The Germans had a formi-
dable word for it: *Quellenscheidung* (the "separation
of sources"). Basically, one distinguished between the
J source, which used YHWH as the divine name, and
which was said to have originated in the Southern
Kingdom; the E source, which used *Elohim* as a name
of God, and which was said to have originated in the
Northern Kingdom; "D," which stands for the Deu-
teronomic Code, representing a good part of our present Book of Deuteronomy, and said to have been the
"book of the *torah*," the finding of which is described
in II Kings, chapter 22 (though scholarship prefers to
speak about the actual writing, rather than the "finding," at that time); and, finally, P, the Priestly Code,
said to contain even post-Exilic material, and specializ-
ing in genealogies (all the "begats" we find in the
Torah) and ceremonial institutions. At one time or
another, one or more of these "sources" were linked
with others, until, after the work of "R" (the "redactor"), all the "sources" were finally combined into one
whole, and accepted as "canonical" by the people. This
is said to have happened around the year 400 B.C.E.

Needless to say, there were no further attempts at
"harmonizing" contradictory passages. The discovery
of such contradictions became, instead, an important
part of biblical scholarship. These contradictions
merely underlined the assumption that one was dealing with "sources" of different origins. As for the narrative portions, each apparent "repetition" of one and

the same story became highly significant. In this way one could trace the manner in which ancient "cultic" legends were retold at *different* sanctuaries.

It must not be forgotten that, in all this post-Mosaic dating of the Pentateuch, one had to reckon with the preaching of several major and minor Prophets *before* the composition of the Torah. The events of the Babylonian Exile, too, were assumed to be reflected in the Torah, while the description of the Tabernacle in the wilderness, in the days of Moses, was said to have been merely a retrojection into the past of the Jerusalem Temple. When "sources" could not be so neatly "separated," one relied on emending the texts, and on designating such passages as were in the way, "later glosses."

Nor did scholarship remain satisfied with J, E, P, and D. By the middle of the twentieth century, Bible critics were operating with the following "sources": J, E, JE, D, D$_1$, C, K, S, Pg, P$_1$, P$_2$, and others. Similar divisions of "sources" were performed on the writings of the Prophets. Here, too, the attempt was made to establish the original text, freed from all later "glosses." The end result was a complete reconstruction of early Jewish history. No longer was it assumed that God revealed the Torah to Moses, and that the Prophets came later to recall a backsliding people to the true way revealed in the days of the fathers. Rather is ethical monotheism presented as a slowly evolving process, —with most of the Prophets waging their warfare against paganism long before the compromise of priestly and prophetic teachings was perpetuated in the canon of the Torah.

Not all modern scholars find it possible to maintain the complete "documentary hypothesis" in the light of more recent findings in such fields as Archaeology and linguistic studies. Thus, provisions of the Torah which, at one time, were assumed to have been post-Exilic, and to date from as late as the fifth century B.C.E., have been found in Babylonian and Hittite law codes centuries and millennia before that time. Much of the early work in the field of *Quellenscheidung* was also predicated on the assumption that the Israelites in the days of Moses could neither read nor write. Such an assumption has turned out to be no longer tenable. Again, one of the basic presuppositions of the Wellhausen school was that of a perpetual conflict between Prophet and Priest. We now know that this presupposition was not a little indebted to Hegelian notions of "thesis" and "antithesis" which were then fashionable in the German academic world. And the discovery that there were actually "cultic prophets," Prophets, that is, who were able to speak their very denunciations within the ritual framework of a temple service, has made us a little more careful in the assertion of neat and clear-cut divisions.

In some quarters, indeed, there has been a recognition of the fact that separating more and more literary "sources" of the Pentateuch from one another can no longer help us very much in learning more about the religious life of ancient Israel. Particularly the Scandinavian scholars have given up the investigation of such *literary* "sources" in favor of tracing the *oral* traditions of early Israel. Long before a literary "source" came into being, so they claim, it must have been preceded by on *oral* tradition. In fact, what written documents we have in the Pentateuch can only be understood in the light of the oral traditions. The "dating" of "documents" alone is seen to be a futile endeavor.

Other scholars, without going to that extreme, have begun to take issue with the particular dates ascribed to "sources" by the Wellhausen school. One such scholar is the Israeli, Yehezkel Kaufmann, who, in his elaborate work on *The History of the Israelite Faith*, claims that, contrary to Wellhausen's hypothesis, the P Code preceded the D Code.

Modern biblical scholarship is a scientific discipline, and is as prone to trial and error as any other discipline. It is constantly changing to keep pace with new evidence and new discoveries. Certainly, biblical scholarship of the middle of the twentieth century is not identical with biblical scholarship of the middle of the nineteenth century. Nor will the state of that scholarship a century hence bear too many resemblances to its present state.

There are, moreover, some vital and important things which we shall probably never know. Perhaps "R," the final "redactor," has done too good a job, after all, in piecing together his various sources. He may well have integrated some of his "sources" in such expert fashion that we do not even suspect their erstwhile separate existence. It would be quite out of keep-

ing with their professed dedication to objective scholarship for any Bible scholars to claim absolute truth
and finality for their particular conclusions.

One conclusion, however, has thus far stood the test
of time, and is liable to do so yet in the future. There
may be disagreements as to the exact scope of the individual "sources." There may be considerable disagreements as to the precise "dating" of these "sources." But
that the Pentateuch is a composite work, that, whether
wholly or partly Mosaic or not, it is, in its final form,
the work of a "redactor" or an editor,—of that there
can be very little doubt. And that fact is of the utmost
significance in our attempt to understand the religious
history of early Israel. There *are* a number of different
legal "codes" within the Pentateuch. There *are* a number of different narratives telling of a covenantal acceptance of *torah* on the part of the people,—both
within the Pentateuch and in other biblical books.

The Historical Approach

And if, by now, the reader should ask, "What has
all this to do with the *meaning* of the Torah for the
modern Jew, with his faith, and with his personal commitment?," then we must respectfully remind him
that, so far, we have been looking at that old "marriage
contract" as interested historians. We have made no
claim to the possession of inside information about the
feeling of the "partners" involved in this "union." We
have looked at this "marriage contract" in very much

the same way in which we would look at others. We have evinced an interest in names, in dates, in places, and in terminology. Such an interest is not to be despised. For whatever the conclusions we might ultimately reach on the basis of a more intimate knowledge and of a personal involvement, the fact remains that we are living in a world where most of our fellowmen are able to approach this particular "marriage contract" only in the capacity of interested historians. And we must be able to understand their language, and to communicate with them.

What the interested historian can see in the Torah may perhaps best be summed up in the following words of Professor Edward Robertson, of the University of Manchester: "The origins of many human institutions are lost in the mists of antiquity, and where man has no certain tradition of origin he ascribes it to a god. . . . It is not surprising that law should be, in respect of antiquity of origin, in the same category as writing. . . . It was commonly accepted by early peoples that it could only have come from heaven for the benefit of man. It was so amongst the ancient Egyptians, and it was so in Babylonia. Everyone is familiar with the stele on which are inscribed the laws associated with the name of Hammurabi. On its upper part is a representation of the Babylonian king in the presence of the Sun-god, the suggestion being that he received his law code, presumably by dictation, from Shamash himself. So it was also in later times with the Greeks and the Romans. . . . Here, too, Hebrew traditions and beliefs are in accord. . . . The sanctifica-

tion of scriptures is a slow-moving but intensely interesting process. Not only must they be concerned
with deity and man's relationship to him, but they
must also be hallowed by time. All trace of human
authorship must be given time to disappear and be forgotten, whilst the contents come to be regarded with an
ever-growing and ever-deepening veneration. From
that stage to an assertion and recognition of divine
authorship is but a step, especially in a community
with a belief in the direct intervention of deity in the
earth process and his participation in the affairs of
men. All this lies behind us in the history of the
Torah." [8]

CHAPTER TWO

Love Letters

A<small>LL</small> that the objective historian can say about the "marriage contract" witnessing to the union of God and Israel has, we believe, been quite fairly summarized in the preceding chapter. What it amounts to is a study of the religious evolution of ancient Israel on the basis of the documents which have survived. Neither the study nor the conclusions differ very much from similar studies and conclusions based on the documents of other ancient peoples. The Egyptians, the Babylonians, the Greeks and the Romans, all have "marriage contracts" of one kind or another to show for themselves. And if our interest in ancient Israel were confined to its *external* history, we could leave it at that,—possibly with some sociological, geographical, and economic hypotheses thrown in for good measure.

But our interest extends beyond that particular horizon. We happen to *be* that Israel, living some two millennia after the completion of the biblical canon, and we endeavor to be vibrant and alive,—and not just a mere "fossil" of an ancient civilization. To know that the ancient Israelites, like all other ancient peoples, ascribed the origin of their law and lore to their national god, because they did not know any better,— that is not quite enough for us. Fortunately, however, we happen to know a little more about the "partners" of that particular "marriage,"—more, indeed, than we know about the Menahem and Flavia who got married in Ancona in the spring of 1723. The fact is that Jewish literature, beginning with the Bible itself, is full of "love letters" which the partners to this particular union have addressed to each other. Yet, since it might well be claimed that the many expressions of the love of God for Israel are not His own actual words, but merely the imagination of men, we shall confine ourselves in this chapter to some of the "love letters" admittedly addressed *by* Israel *to* God. Moreover, we shall make our selection from those "love letters" only which have some bearing on the subject of Torah, so that, through them, the bare text of the Torah, which we considered in the last chapter, may come to life for us.

Torah in the Psalms

The Book of Psalms is the hymn book of biblical Israel. In it the singer voices his, and his people's, deepest longings and highest aspirations. Verse after verse speaks of God's love for Israel, and of Israel's love for God. It is characteristic, then, that this Book of Psalms not only begins with a poem praising the man whose "delight is in the *torah* of the LORD," (Psalm 1:2) but that it also contains a chapter of 176 verses—the longest chapter in the Bible—devoted to the praise of the Torah. We are speaking of Psalm 119. Its 176 verses are due to the fact that eight verses each begin with every single one of the 22 letters of the Hebrew alphabet. We might say that it was the psalmist's intention to praise God and the Torah "from A to Z";—and not only once, but eight times! Here are some of the verses:—

> With my whole heart have I sought Thee;
> O let me not err from Thy commandments. (10)

> Blessed art Thou, O LORD;
> Teach me Thy statutes. (12)

> Open Thou mine eyes, that I may behold
> Wondrous things out of Thy *torah*. (18)

> I am a sojourner in the earth;
> Hide not Thy commandments from me. (19)

> Remove from me the way of falsehood;
> And favor me with Thy *torah*. (29)

> Give me understanding, that I keep Thy *torah*
> And observe it with my whole heart. (34)

> Behold, I have longed after Thy precepts;
> Quicken me in Thy righteousness. (40)

The bands of the wicked have enclosed me;
But I have not forgotten Thy *torah*.   (61)

The earth, O LORD, is full of Thy mercy;
Teach me Thy statutes.   (64)

The *torah* of Thy mouth is better unto me
Than thousands of gold and silver.   (72)

Unless Thy *torah* had been my delight,
I should then have perished in mine affliction.   (92)

Oh how I love Thy *torah!*
It is my meditation all the day.   (97)

I have longed for Thy salvation, O LORD;
And Thy *torah* is my delight.   (174)

Another hymn in praise of the Torah is found in Psalm 19:—

The *torah* of the LORD is perfect;
Restoring the soul;

The testimony of the LORD is sure,
Making wise the simple.

The precepts of the LORD are right,
Rejoicing the heart;

The commandment of the LORD is pure,
Enlightening the eyes.

The fear of the LORD is clean,
Enduring for ever;

The ordinances of the LORD are true,
They are righteous altogether;

More to be desired are they than gold,
Yea, than much fine gold;
Sweeter also than honey and the honeycomb.

(Verses 8-11.)

As will be recalled, the beginning of Psalm 19 does not deal with the Torah at all, but with the idea of God's glory in nature. "The heavens declare the glory of God, and the firmament showeth His handiwork." It is quite possible that the two sections of this psalm were originally separate poems, joined together at a later time by an editor. Yet the combination of the two ideas, of Nature and of Torah, was a happy one, and it has remained a characteristic of Judaism ever since.

In the Liturgy

When the *Shema* ("the watchword of our faith") is recited in a Jewish worship service, it is always surrounded by a number of blessings (that is: prayers concluding with the phrase, "Praised art Thou, O LORD, . . ."). There are two blessings before the *Shema*, and, in the morning service, there is one blessing following the *Shema*, and, in the evening service, two. The blessing immediately following the *Shema* in both morning and evening services always expresses the idea of Redemption. Mention is made of the liberation from

Egyptian slavery, and the hope is voiced for the messianic redemption of the future.

While the blessing after the *Shema* thus deals with Redemption, the two blessings before the *Shema* express the ideas of "God in Nature" and of "Torah" respectively. If, instead of "God in Nature" and "Torah," we were to use the terms "Creation" and "Revelation," we would find that the daily rubric of "the *Shema* and its blessings" bears out the pattern which Franz Rosenzweig (1886/1929) saw in Judaism, and which he described in his monumental work, *The Star of Redemption*. Rosenzweig starts out with the three basic entities of religion: God, Man, and the World. He finds the nature of Judaism in the manner in which it conceives of the links between these entities. God is linked to the World by means of the act of Creation. God is linked to Man by means of the act of Revelation. And Man's relation to the World is seen in terms of the process of Redemption.

In the morning service, the first blessing before the *Shema* praises God, "who giveth light to the earth and to them that dwell thereon, and who, in His mercy, daily reneweth the work of creation." The corresponding blessing in the evening service praises God, "who bringeth on the evening twilight." Both of these blessings, as was mentioned already, are followed by a blessing dealing with the Torah, or rather, with God's love for Israel, which manifests itself in Israel's possession of the Torah. We quote here the form of this blessing which is recited in the evening. Some of the ideas ex-

pressed in it will be considered in greater detail in the
following chapters:—

> With everlasting love
> Hast Thou loved the House of Israel, Thy People;
> Torah and commandments,
> Statutes and judgments,
> Hast Thou taught us.

> Therefore,
> O LORD our God,
> When we lie down,
> And when we rise up,
> We will speak of Thy statutes,
> And rejoice in the words of Thy Torah,
> And in Thy commandments,
> For ever and aye.

> For they are our life
> And the length of our days;
> Day and night will we meditate on them.

> As for Thy love,
> Mayest Thou never remove it from us.

> Praised art Thou, O LORD,
> Lover of His people Israel.

The Torah figures not only in the prayers which are
part of the standard liturgy for every day, that is to say,
in the prayers which the pious Jew is *required* to re-
cite. If this were so, and if such were the only "love
letters" at our disposal, then the thoroughgoing skeptic
might still question the sincerity and the spontaneity

of the sentiments expressed. But we do find constant references to the Torah also in the *private* prayers which the great teachers of the past used to offer up to God after the conclusion of the prescribed liturgy. One example of this type of prayer must suffice here. The Talmud [1] quotes it as the personal prayer of Rabbi Ḥiyyah:—

> May it be Thy will,
> O LORD our God,
> That Thy Torah be our skill;
> So that our heart may not be sad,
> Nor our eyes darkened.

Rejoicing in the Torah

In this connection, too, we should mention the Festival of "Rejoicing in the Torah," which is celebrated at the end of Sukkoth. It is a festival of which there is no trace in either Bible or Talmud. Indeed, as Robert Gordis has shown,[2] this is a festival which the *people* themselves created in the Middle Ages. Its joyful observance,[3] its mirthful customs, its dances and songs, and even its overriding of some of the rabbinic provisions for that day, were all introduced by popular demand,—over the objections of some of the legal authorities. Only a people which knew itself ever more closely bound to its God through life in the Torah could thus celebrate the day on which they concluded the synagogue reading of Deuteronomy, and began again the reading of Genesis,—books, it will be re-

called, in which the objective outsider can see nothing
but the various edited strata of ancient Hebrew cultural and religious development. But the people who
instituted the Festival of "Rejoicing in the Torah"
were people accustomed to say as one of the first things
every morning:—

> Make pleasant,
> O LORD our God,
> The words of Thy Torah
> In our mouth,
> And in the mouth of Thy people, the House of Israel.

> May we and our offspring,
> And the offspring of Thy people, the House of Israel,
> All of us,
> Know Thy Name,
> And learn Thy Torah.

> Praised art Thou, O LORD,
> Who teachest Torah to Thy people Israel.[4]

The Torah Blessing

Here, then, are a few of the "love letters" composed throughout the course of Jewish history, which
may shed some light on what was really involved in
that "union" between God and Israel of which the
Torah is the official "marriage contract." We have endeavored to let the "love letters" speak for themselves,
and to let the reader form his own reactions to their
content. We must now consider some of their phrase-

ology in some greater detail, in order to determine the meaning and the relevance of Torah for the modern Jew. To do so, we shall take as our starting-point the blessing which is recited prior to the reading of the Scripture Lesson in the synagogue:—

Praised art Thou,
O LORD, our God, Sovereign of the Universe,
Who hast chosen us from all peoples,
And hast given us Thy Torah.

Praised art Thou, O LORD,
Giver of the Torah.

CHAPTER THREE

"Lord, Our God, Sovereign of the Universe"

JEWISHLY speaking, the concept of Torah is meaningless if it is divorced from the belief in God. Torah is the result (in whatever form we may conceive of it) of an act of divine revelation. What Torah means to us will, therefore, very much depend on what God means to us.

It is relatively easy to speak in general terms about "the Jewish idea of God." But it ceases to be quite as simple once we ask: What does Judaism *mean* by God? Is there, in fact, a uniform God concept among all Jews of all the ages? Put this way, the question can immediately be answered in the negative. The highly abstract concept of God held by Maimonides (1135/1204) was not identical with some of the more anthropomorphic (i.e., speaking of God in human and physical terms) views held by many of his predecessors

and contemporaries. The "Sweet Father" whom the
Hasidic *Zaddik* addressed in an outburst of religious
enthusiasm had little in common with the Neo-Kan-
tian "Guarantor of our Ethics,"—which is the way
Hermann Cohen (1842/1918) conceived of God.

The Unity of God

Yet all Jews have ever united in confessing at least
this: that God is One! Perhaps it is this declaration of
the Unity of God, and it alone, which permits us to
speak at all about *the* Jewish concept of God. It is this
that makes the *Shema* ("Hear, O Israel, the LORD our
God, the LORD is One!") the "watchword of our faith."
For the *Shema* expresses the Jew's conviction that,
though he may experience God in many different
spheres and on many different levels, all his different
and diverse experiences are nonetheless the manifestations of the same One God. And—this needs stressing—
the Jew *does* deal with manifestations of the Divine
on different levels. This is a truth already taught in the
Bible. In Exodus 6:2ff. we read that *Elohim* ("God")
revealed Himself to Moses as YHWH ("the LORD"), stating at the same time that the Patriarchs, Abraham,
Isaac, and Jacob, had not known Him under this aspect, but only as *El Shaddai* ("God Almighty").

Now this passage, the springboard for many a theological discussion, clearly implies much more than a
mere change of name. Names have meanings. And
there is more than a mere difference in nomenclature

between the three divine names mentioned in this passage. Whatever the original significance of these names, and their provenance within the framework of Semitic religion, this passage evidently indicates that the authors of the Bible were not unaware of the different levels on which God is experienced, or of the different aspects under which He is known. Yet, strictly speaking, all three of them have now—perhaps, on account of that very revelation—become synonyms for the One God of biblical religion. The point Judaism is making, the message of the *Shema,* is that all these levels and aspects are manifestations of the same One God.

"God of Aristotle" and "God of Abraham"

A similar recognition was forced upon the medieval Jewish philosophers, who were acquainted, on the one hand, with the Aristotelian-scholastic "proofs for the existence of God," and, on the other, with the "revealed" God of the Scriptures. Judah Halevi (ca. 1080/1140) is quite outspoken in the distinction he makes between the "God of Aristotle" and the "God of Abraham." [1] For the Jewish thinker there can, of course, be only One God, and he will have to insist that the philosopher and the prophet speak about the same Deity,—adding, however, that "revelation" can give us certitude where mere philosophical speculation may not. This kind of approach worked out very nicely as long as the sciences and metaphysics were satisfied to remain in their rôle as handmaidens to Theology. But there came a time when the handmaidens broke loose and made themselves independent, when Philosophy began to operate with concepts of "God" to which Theology could find no inner relation at all. And this is the situation in which we find ourselves today.

Inasmuch as the Jew today describes himself as "believing in God," he would own up to some philosophical God concept or other,—a concept which will be used to make sense of, or to account for, the universe. In a way, it will be something like the "law of gravity." We invoke it to explain to ourselves a certain phenomenon. But it is nothing that will inspire man with reverence, or wring from man's lips words of adoration. The "God concept" we invoke by way of making sense, or trying to make sense, of the universe, is not identical with the biblical "God Who hearkens to prayer." It is also not the God with Whom one can associate the "revelation" of Torah.

The God of Israel

It will, however, be conceded that Judaism, as a historical phenomenon, did not grow out of a philosophical God concept. Judah Halevi saw this very clearly, when he pointed out that the first of the Ten Commandments does *not* say: "I am the LORD, thy God, Who created heaven and earth." But it *does* say: "I am the LORD, thy God, Who brought thee out of the land of Egypt, out of the house of bondage." [2] In other words, while the "God of the Philosophers" is a concept which must be kept in very broad and universal terms, the "God of Israel" is a God Whose existence and nature were made manifest to Israel in certain historical situations of a more or less well defined character.

The liberation from Egypt was one such event. The "passing through the Red Sea" was another;—and so throughout Jewish history. One of these historical situations was the "standing at Mount Sinai." It was here that Israel entered into a covenant relationship with God. The God Who had revealed Himself as the Author of Liberty in the Exodus, now revealed Himself as the Author of Torah at Sinai. What is more, He manifested a special interest in the people of Israel, who were henceforth to describe themselves as His "chosen people."

Is all this legendary? Many describe it as such. But if so, then for the past two and a half millennia and more the Jews have been victims of a very clever deception— a deception, moreover, for which generations after generations risked persecution and martyrdom. After all, Judah Halevi's argument is not so easily refuted. When he tries to prove the authenticity of the Sinaitic Revelation by calling attention to the fact that 600,000 Israelites actually witnessed it,[3] we may, if we like, quibble about his statistics. But it still remains a *fact* that the people, as a whole, in view of certain experiences they had undergone, accepted certain obligations as part of their covenant commitment.

It must be said, therefore, that if the "God Idea" has been a dynamic factor in Jewish life and history at all (and who could possibly deny that?!), then it was precisely the "God of Israel," the God Who led the ancestors out of Egypt, Who revealed His Torah, and Who watched over His people throughout their many wanderings. There have been attempts to make light of the belief in the "God of Israel" by referring to Him (and dismissing Him) as merely a "reported God." Such attempts ignore the fact that in Judaism the "reported God" ever and again becomes a very present reality. This is made clear, to take but one example out of many, in Psalm 106. In forty-six verses this Psalm recounts ("reports") the past dealings of God with Israel. And, after mention has been made of God's remembering His covenant, the Psalm reaches its climax in verse 47 (verse 48 is no longer part of this Psalm, but the concluding doxology of the Fourth Book of Psalms): "Save us, O LORD our God, and gather us from among the nations . . ." It was, after all, the "reported God" of historical tradition Who alone held out hopes of *present* salvation!

The Shekhinah

But it was not only in the past that God manifested Himself. There is also the religious experience of the *present*. Judaism has a word for it: *Shekhinah,* "The indwelling presence of God." We might say that the personal religious experience of the individual—

and not only that of the mystic—is a manifestation of *Shekhinah*.

There are, then, at least three aspects to the God-head of which Judaism knows, though their full number might well be infinite. Regard them as completely distinct from one another, and you leave the confines of Judaism. Regard them as the different levels on which man can experience God, and you adhere to the Confession of Unity expressed in the *Shema*. This means, of course, that when you experience God on any one level, you must never completely leave out of account the various other levels on which God *can* be experienced. Thus, the mystical experience of God vouchsafed to an Israel Ba'al Shem Tov, the founder of Hasidism (1700/1760), may be peculiarly his very own. But a Ba'al Shem Tov would insist that the God he has encountered is none other than the God of Israel's history, since there is, after all, only One God. Again, the God Who, as Saadia Gaon (892/942) thinks, can be proved by logical reasoning is, for this philoso-pher, none other than the One Who revealed Himself at Sinai. Or, to take an example from the opposite ex-treme, the *élan vital*, discovered by Henri Bergson (1859/1941) through his biological and philosophical researches, is recognized by him to be the very source of *mystical* experience, whose existence is attested to by a long line of religious mystics.

If, then, we insist that the characteristically *Jewish* approach to the belief in God is the stress on His *Unity*, we would fail to do justice to this very concept were we to deny the possibility of the various levels of authentic religious knowledge and experience which this belief is meant to *unify*. In other words, if "God" is only that which appears at the end of my chain of logical reasoning, and not also the "God of Israel" and the *Shekhinah,* the "reported God" and the God of personal religious experience, what meaning could there possibly be in stressing the *Unity* of God?!

An appreciation of these various levels is an absolute prerequisite for our understanding of Torah, of the Teaching and Law emanating from God. We have already seen that the revelation of Torah is something that cannot very well be associated with the "God of the Philosophers." But then, as has been shown, the "God of the Philosophers" by no means exhausts the Divine as understood by Judaism. The road of speculation is, after all, but *one* avenue through which the Jew may receive intimations of the Divine. And, while the "God of the Philosophers" may not reveal Torah, the "God of Israel" certainly does! If, however, it be argued that the "God of Israel" is only a "reported God" who has no immediate relevance to the present-day Jew, Judaism would answer that an experience of *Shekhinah* is within reach of all; [4] and to the Jew an experience of *Shekhinah* carries overtones of the other aspects of God as well.

Now, it is obvious that an experience of *Shekhinah* is a very subjective state. Here we are moving in the realm of what William James called *The Varieties of Religious Experience.* One would naturally be very wary of regarding every subjective state of spiritual elation, every "vision," or feeling of being "reborn," as authentic manifestations of God! That is where the Jewish belief in the Unity of God comes in, with its insistence on the *identity* of *Shekhinah* with the "God of Israel." The Jew's experience of the one serves, as it were, as a "check" on the validity of the experience of the other. We have no doubt, for example, that the so-called "false prophets" of Bible days had their religious experiences, their "visions," and their "revelations." What made their prophecy "false" in the eyes of the "true" Prophets was that the happy prognostications they offered—unconnected as they were with any moral task and call to ethical improvement—were felt to be out of keeping with the character of Israel's God Who had revealed Himself in history.[5]

To sum up, the Unity of God, as proclaimed in the *Shema*, means that there is only *one* God, though we may get to know Him, or about Him, by diverse routes: by philosophical speculation, by tradition, and by personal religious experience. No *one* approach, however, is self-sufficient. Neither philosophical speculation alone, nor yet a personal religious "experience," will reveal to us the full implications of what God means in Judaism. The "God of Israel," faith in the God Whom Israel encountered in history, is that aspect of the Jewish experience of God which provides the continuity within Judaism, and which makes it possible for us to link the Torah with God.

Adonai, Our Elohim

It is certainly no accident that the Torah Blessing, with which we concluded our last chapter, invokes God as "LORD, our God, Sovereign of the Universe,"—or, to be a little more accurate, as "YHWH, our *Elohim,* Sovereign of the Universe." *Elohim,* in Hebrew, denotes a superhuman power or powers. It depends upon the context in which it is found whether the word is to be translated as God, god, gods, angels, or even, occasionally, as (human) judges. To the extent to which a man recognizes a force above him, to that extent he may be said to have an *elohim.* Naturally, from the perspective of any one religion, there is (or are) the "true" *elohim* and the "strange" *elohim.* As the psalmist puts it: "For all the *elohim* of the peoples are things of nought; but the LORD made the heavens." (Psalm 96:5.) To say, therefore, that one has an *elohim* does not yet convey any information about the nature of his religion,—any more than a modern man's statement that he believes in God offers us any key to the *kind* of God in whom he believes. If, then, we were to say that the Bible, or the Rabbis, inculcated belief in *elohim,* or in "God," we would be making a true statement, but one which is in need of further explanation.

That is why Judaism maintains that YHWH is our *elohim,* and why the Torah Blessing is addressed to "YHWH, our *Elohim.*" The name YHWH (which we Jews read as *Adonai,* and which is commonly translated as "the LORD") is, as we have already seen, the Name revealed to Moses at the beginning of his mission. (Exodus 6:2ff.) The Name is connected with the Hebrew word *HaYaH* or *HaWaH,* which means "to be"; and it is for this reason that some vernacular versions of the Bible translate this Name as "the Eternal."

However, as Martin Buber has shown,[6] the Hebrew word *HaYaH* is not an abstract word, carrying philosophical overtones of "eternal being." Rather has it the sense of "happening, coming into being, being there, being present." The Divine Name, therefore, has to be understood in the light of such verses as Exodus 3:12, "And He said: 'Certainly, I will be with thee. . . .'" And when, in Exodus 3:14, God gives His Name as *Ehyeh Asher Ehyeh* (etymologically connected with YHWH), it does not mean, as it is commonly translated, "I Am that I Am," but rather: "I am and remain present." As a matter of fact, this is already the interpretation we find in the Talmud, where God's words in Exodus 3:14 are paraphrased as "Just as I was with you in the present enslavement, so shall I always be with you when foreign kingdoms enslave you in the future." [7]

"The LORD," then, is the God Who is present in concrete historical situations, the God Who is manifest in Israel's history. *Elohim*, unqualified, may become a philosophical abstraction. But YHWH as *Elohim* is the God Who cares, and Israel's possession of the Torah is evidence of this care.

Yet our Torah Blessing also describes Him as "Sovereign of the Universe." This description, too, is not without its significance for our concept of Torah. There have been concepts of God in the history of human thought which envisaged God as the great Clockmaker. God made this universe in very much the same way in which a clockmaker manufactures a clock. And, just as the clockmaker, when the clock has been finished, winds it up, and forgets about it, so God, after He had set this universe in motion, retired from it, and lost all further interest in the affairs of men. Judaism, on the other hand, conceives of God as the sovereign, the ruler, of the universe, Who is very much concerned with the moral government of this world. Judaism could not be *"Ethical* Monotheism" if it did not posit God's *continued* government, and His *abiding* concern with the moral welfare of mankind.

But if such is indeed God's concern, it follows that there must be some way in which God makes known His Will to mankind. A ruler who is held *incommunicado* cannot very well exercise his rulership to any effect. The concept of the "Sovereign of the Universe" in Judaism, therefore, inevitably leads to the concept of Torah, to the revelation of God's Will to man.

To summarize: As Jews we approach the Torah with a prayer of thanksgiving addressed to "the Lord, our God, Sovereign of the Universe." The implications of this are that the God we thus address is not a mere philosophical abstraction, but the ever-present God of Israel's historical experience, and that this God, as Sovereign of the Universe, has seen fit to reveal His Will to man.

To stress the "God of Israel" as an aspect of Deity does not mean that Judaism rules out philosophical speculation, or discountenances the religious experience of the individual. Indeed, the very proclamation of the *Shema* is evidence not only of our belief in the Divine Unity, but also of our awareness that there are different levels on which God is experienced,—levels which the belief in Unity is meant to *unify,* to relate to one and the same Source.

In terms of our investigation into the meaning of Torah this means that the Jew who is unable to relate Torah to his philosophical "God concept" has not yet exhausted the realm of the Divine as understood by Judaism. The "God of the Philosophers" is but one avenue, one pointer, to that Divine Unity which includes also *Shekhinah,* the manifestation of God to the individual in personal religious experience, and the "God of Israel," the One Who "is and remains present," and Who, as our succeeding chapters will attempt to show, is the source and the inspiration of Torah.

CHAPTER FOUR

Who Hast Chosen Us

AFTER addressing "the LORD, our God, Sovereign of the Universe," the Torah Blessing goes on to say: "Who hast chosen us from all peoples, and hast given us Thy Torah." In these few words we have an expression not only of the thought that the "chosen people" concept is an inseparable part of the idea of Torah, but also of the obverse: that the concept of the "chosen people" can only be understood in terms of Torah. Once this basic fact is grasped, much misunderstanding will be prevented. And yet, the idea that God *chose* Israel is not, at first blush, an easy one to grasp, and one to elicit modern man's assent. In fact, it is an idea which has to be treated on various and different levels.

On one level, indeed, it is quite uncomplicated. Given the biblical Israel, given furthermore their awareness that their religion was something new, something different, something not shared by their contem-

poraries, and given, too, their belief that this something
new and different was also God's Truth,—and it must
needs follow that a special act of divine favor was shown
to Israel, that Israel was *chosen* by God.

Biblical Israel

"Only in Israel did an ethical monotheism exist,"
the late Dr. Leo Baeck wrote,[1] "and wherever else it is
found later on, it has been derived directly or indirectly
from Israel. The existence of this form of religion was
conditioned by the existence of the people of Israel,
and so Israel became one of the nations that have a
mission to fulfill. That is what is called the *election* of
Israel. Hence this word expresses primarily only an
historical fact, it defines an essential specific peculiar-
ity which has here come to the front. It indicates the
fact that there was assigned to this people a peculiar
position in the world, that it achieved something which
distinguished it from all the other nations."

But if the word expresses primarily only an historical
fact, it is still a fact in a history which, biblically speaking, is the history of God's redemptive acts, of God's
dealings with Israel. That is why the Torah introduces
the subject of the "election," of God's choice of Israel,
with the following words:—

"Ye have seen what I did to the Egyptians,
and how I bore you on eagles' wings,
and brought you unto Myself.
Now therefore,

if ye will hearken unto My voice indeed,
and keep My covenant,
then ye shall be Mine own treasure from among all
    peoples;
for all the earth is Mine.
And ye shall be unto Me a kingdom of priests,
and a holy nation.
These are the words which thou shalt speak unto the
    children of Israel."

(Exodus 19:4-6.)

God elected Israel in order to make a covenant with
Israel. Of course, it takes two to make a covenant, to
enter into a treaty. The objective historian, therefore,
looking at the matter from the *human* angle, is not
wrong if he speaks in terms of Israel's choosing YHWH
as its God, and, consequently, deeming itself to be
YHWH's "chosen people." Israel undoubtedly made a
choice,—the kind of choice which they again made in
the days of Joshua, and of which the twenty-fourth
chapter of the Book of Joshua gives us such a detailed
description.

A Covenant in Shechem

Said Joshua to the people: "Now therefore fear
the LORD, and serve Him in sincerity and in truth;
and put away the gods which your fathers served beyond the River, and in Egypt; and serve ye the LORD.
But if it seem evil to you to serve the LORD, choose
you this day whom ye will serve; whether the gods

which your fathers served that were beyond the River, or the gods of the Amorites, in whose land ye dwell. But as for me and my house, we will serve the LORD."

And the people answered and said: "Far be it from us that we should forsake the LORD, to serve other gods; for the LORD our God, He it is that brought us and our fathers up out of the land of Egypt, from the house of bondage. . . ."

Yet Joshua warned them of the dangers connected with the choice they were making. The LORD does not tolerate idol worship. He is a jealous God. Still, the people insisted: "Nay, but we will serve the LORD!"

Then Joshua said unto the people: "Ye are witnesses against yourselves that ye have chosen you the LORD, to serve Him." (And they said: "We are witnesses!") "Now therefore put away the strange gods which are among you, and incline your heart unto the LORD, the God of Israel." (And the people said to Joshua: "The LORD our God will we serve, and unto His voice will we hearken.")

So Joshua made a covenant with the people that day, and set them a statute and an ordinance in Shechem.

The picture is quite clear. The people saw in the experiences of their immediate past the work of the LORD. Given the choice, they chose the LORD as their God, rather than the ancestral pagan deities. They bound themselves to this LORD. This implied the removal of all traces of paganism and other religious allegiances. It meant ordering their daily lives from the perspective of the Rulership of the LORD. And it also meant that the "other Party" to this covenant would henceforth act as this people's Protector.

This much, as we have said, is evident to the objective historian. The facts he reads in the Book of Joshua easily lend themselves to a reconstruction of the analogous events said to have taken place in the days of Moses,—particularly so, because the entering into a covenant relationship by deities and peoples is also known from other documents which have survived from the religions of the ancient Near and Middle East.

"Thou hast let the LORD say this day that He is thy God, . . . And the LORD hath let thee say this day that thou art a people for His own possession." (Deuteronomy 26:17-18.) That is the way the "election," the making of the covenant, on the level we are discussing at the moment, is described in the Torah. And the Rabbis of the Talmud elaborate this statement by making God say to Israel: "You have made Me *your* choice object in this world (as it is said, Deuteronomy 6:4, 'Hear, O Israel, the LORD our God, the LORD is *One.*'); therefore will I make you *My* choice object in the world (as it is said, I Chronicles 17:21, 'And who is like Thy people Israel, a nation *one* in the earth?')." [2]

The underlying thought of passages like that is quite in consonance with what modern historical scholarship has to say on the subject. Here, for example, is what Professor Theodore H. Robinson writes: "It may be taken for granted that the tribes—or such of them as Moses had collected—worshipped different gods, and his task was to introduce them to the cult of a new deity, who should combine them into a single whole from the religious, and so from every other point of view. It was inevitable that the God chosen for the

purpose should be He whom Moses had learnt to know
during his exile, He who had given Moses his com-
mission." [3] In other words, for purposes of national
unity (according to Professor Robinson), or for military reasons (according to such scholars as Professor
Budde), Israel *needed* a new God, and what was known
about the character of YHWH, Who, according to some
scholars, was originally the deity of the Kenite tribe in
Midian,[4] eminently suited Him to fill that rôle. And,
after YHWH was chosen by Israel, Israel, of necessity,
became YHWH's "chosen people."

The Prophetic Ideal

If, in their tribal phase, this is really the way in
which the "covenant" appeared to the people of Israel,
it certainly cannot be said that this is the Bible's last
word on this subject. In the thought of the Prophets,
Israel is the people which God "formed for Himself,
that they might tell of His praise." (Isaiah 43:21.)
Here, clearly, the initiative is conceived of as resting
with *God*. The same Prophet makes it quite clear
what the "election" means to him:—

> "Ye are My witnesses,
> saith the LORD,
> And My servant whom I have chosen;
> That ye may know and believe Me, and understand
> That I am He;
> Before Me there was no God formed,
> Neither shall any be after Me."

> (Isaiah 43:10.)

And it is in this sense, too, that we must understand the speech, quoted above, about God's bearing Israel on eagles' wings, and bringing them unto Himself;— the speech charging Israel with becoming a kingdom of priests and a holy nation. God has taken the initiative. The God Who can say, "all the earth is Mine," Who has created the earth, and Who has an aim for this earth,—this God picked Israel as His "own treasure from among all peoples," to be unto Him "a kingdom of priests." Here is "election" as seen from the perspective of God. Here is where the results of objective historical scholarship must needs differ from the basic convictions of faith. The former is confined to what the historical realities show about the "what" and the "how" of the workings out of an idea. The latter claims to have a knowledge of the idea itself.

Ideas do not work in a vacuum. If the destiny of the world is that time when "the earth shall be full of the knowledge of the LORD as the waters cover the sea," (Isaiah 11:9) then the idea of the Kingdom of God must have its *bearers,* its protagonists, its missionaries. And it was for this that Israel was *chosen.*

Israel and the Nations

Why Israel? And what about the other nations?

No doubt, the awareness of being God's "chosen people" could, and did, give rise to feelings of national self-glorification. Surely, there must have been merit in Israel to be thus chosen! But this kind of boasting was easily squelched by the Torah: "For thou art a holy people unto the Lord thy God: the Lord thy God hath chosen thee to be His own treasure, out of all peoples that are upon the face of the earth. The Lord did not set His love upon you, nor choose you, because ye were more in number than any people—for ye were the fewest of all peoples—but because the Lord loved you, and because He would keep the oath which He swore unto your fathers . . ." (Deuteronomy 7:6-8.) Not Israel's merit, but God's love for the few, the downtrodden and the persecuted, and God's promise to the pious Patriarchs,—that was the reason (if "reason" it can be called) for the choice of Israel.

And just as the "choice" was not due to Israel's merit, so did it not imply privilege, but service and responsibility. "I have known you more intimately than all the families of the earth," Amos said in the name of God to his smug, self-satisfied contemporaries; *"therefore* will I visit upon you all your iniquities." (Amos 3:2.) In fact, what glories there have been in Israel's long history have almost exclusively been spiritual glories. In the world of nations and empires, Israel was truly the "Suffering Servant of the Lord." With a profound insight into what the choice of Israel really meant, the ancient Rabbis told of the pre-natal dialogue which took place between Jacob (the ancestor of Israel) and Esau (the incarnation of all that is "un-Jewish"). Jacob said to Esau: "Esau, my brother! We are two brothers, and two worlds lie before us,—this world and the World-to-Come. . . . If you desire, do take this world; and I shall take the World-to-Come." [5] And the outcome of that agreement was surely known already to the heathen prophet Balaam, who said of Israel:

Lo, it is a people that shall dwell alone,
And shall not be reckoned among the nations.
(Numbers 23:9.)

Yet that loneliness of Israel may itself have been as much a cause as it was a consequence of the "election." As Hermann Cohen commented on the words of Balaam just quoted: "The loneliness of Israel must needs lead also to statelessness. But with this their social affliction begins, their social analogy to poverty. Only now does the thought clearly come into its own: that God must love Israel, an isolated people, in its affliction. For this historical affliction of a people without a state can surely compete with social poverty. That is why, in its history, Israel is a prototype of suffering, a symbol of human suffering, of the nature of man. In the love of God for Israel, no less than in His love for the poor, there is expressed the love of God for humankind." [6]

Anti-Semitism

It is but a small step from seeing Jewish suffering as a consequence, or a cause, of the "election" to seeing in Jewish suffering a *proof* for the reality of that "election." That step is implied in the talmudic statement that the mountain of the revelation was called *Sinai* "because from it originated the hatred (*sin-ah*) which

the idolaters feel for Israel." [7] It is expressed even more
explicitly in Franz Rosenzweig's remark: "My 'proof'
for Revelation is not the uniqueness of the Sabbath,
but the uniqueness of—anti-Semitism." [8] And, without
any supernatural overtones, it is still discernible in
Sigmund Freud's explanation of anti-Semitism: "We
must not forget that all the peoples who now excel in
the practice of anti-Semitism became Christians only
in relatively recent times, sometimes forced to it by
bloody compulsion. One might say they are all 'badly
christened'; under the thin veneer of Christianity they
have remained what their ancestors were, barbarically
polytheistic. They have not yet overcome their grudge
against the new religion which was forced on them, and
they have projected it on to *the source from which
Christianity came to them.*" [9]

Still, if sufferance is the badge of all our tribe, if the
"election" has brought us to the stage where we have
to say of God that

> "He hath not made us like the nations of the world,
> Nor placed us like the families of the earth.
> He hath not set our portion like theirs,
> Nor our destiny like that of all their multitude,"
>
> ('*Alenu* Prayer)

there is yet enough glory and satisfaction in the knowledge of being the "chosen people" for the Jew to re-
iterate in joy on festival after festival:

> "Thou hast chosen us from among all peoples.
> Thou hast loved us and taken pleasure in us,
> And Thou hast exalted us above all tongues.

Thou hast sanctified us by Thy commandments,
And Thou hast brought us near, O our King, unto Thy
    service;
And Thou hast called us by Thy great and holy Name."
(Festival 'Amidah)

Election and Rejection

But as soon as the thought of "choice," of "exalta-
tion," and of "bringing near," is contemplated with
any degree of consistency, the question of God's relation to the *other* peoples immediately arises. Does
"election" of one imply "rejection" of the others? If
so, how can this concept be reconciled with the belief
in a just and loving Father of all Mankind? One modern Jewish writer does indeed claim that "election
involves rejection," and, being dedicated to the American democratic ideal, he reaches the conclusion that
"we are . . . constrained to deny that any religious
society or communion is 'chosen,' and to affirm, of
religions as of individuals, the democratic faith that
all of them are created equal; none is chosen and none
rejected." [10]

It is curious that in America, of all places, "election"
should be held to imply "rejection." Our whole system of government is based on "elections." If John
Doe, rather than Joe Smith, gets elected to an office,
it does not mean at all that Joe Smith, *as a person*, is
"rejected," or that the concept of the equality of all
men is thereby denied. It simply means that, in the

view of the electorate, John Doe is more suited for the particular office than the other candidate. Joe Smith has indeed not been elected to the particular office; yet, in the eyes of the law, he is in no way inferior to John Doe.

This analogy becomes particularly relevant once we realize, a point to be taken up later on, that Judaism does not speak of "election" *per se,* but of "election *for* something."* It is, as we have already seen, a question of "Thou hast chosen us . . . and given us Thy Torah," or of "Thou hast chosen us . . . , Thou hast sanctified us by Thy commandments, and Thou hast brought us near . . . to Thy service." And even so, the choice of Israel as God's "priest people" is far from implying that God has had no dealings with other peoples.

True enough, in a moment of enthusiasm, the lawgiver might say unto his people: "Did ever a people hear the voice of God speaking out of the midst of the fire, as thou hast heard, and live?" (Deuteronomy 4:33.) A psalmist could even triumphantly exclaim:

> He declareth His word unto Jacob,
> His statutes and His ordinances unto Israel.
> He hath not dealt so with any nation;
> And as for His ordinances, they have not known them.
> Hallelujah.
>
> (Psalm 147:19-20.)

But the Bible itself knows of God's dealings with Adam and with Noah (both of them non-Jews!), and of the covenant which God made with Noah and his sons (Genesis 9:1-17), which, in effect, was a covenant with the ancestors of all mankind. Rabbinic tradition even knows of the obligations which were implied by this covenant for the "sons of Noah," obligations which, if kept, entitle the Gentile to his share in the World-to-Come. Tradition lists the "Seven Commandments of the Sons of Noah" as: the prohibitions of idolatry, of immorality, of murder, of blasphemy, of theft, and of eating part of a living animal, and the commandment to establish courts of law.[11] It is significant that the famous English jurist, John Selden (1584/1654), identified his concept of Natural Law (*jus naturale et gentium*) with the Noachitic Laws of the Jewish tradition.[12]

Even more remarkable is the rabbinic comment on Deuteronomy 34:10 ("And there hath not arisen a prophet since in Israel like unto Moses, whom the LORD knew face to face."): "In Israel there did not arise a prophet like unto Moses, but among the nations such a one did arise. And who is this? Balaam, the son of Beor." [13] And concerning the very Revelation at Sinai, the Rabbis asked the question, "Why was the Torah given in the wilderness?," and they answered it by saying that "just as the wilderness—being no-man's land—is free to all, so the words of the Torah are free to all the dwellers on earth." [14] Indeed, the Voice of God came forth in seventy languages, "so that all the nations should hear." [15]

In point of historical fact, however, the nations did not heed that Voice. Israel knew itself to be alone and unique. How, then, could they account for that state of affairs? They did so by imagining that God, as it were, hawked around His Torah to the various nations of the world. But every single nation found in that Torah some prohibition or other which would interfere with its national character, with its accustomed way of life. And so, the various nations rejected the Torah. Only, as a kind of last resort, did God offer the Torah to Israel. And Israel, without even inquiring into its contents, gladly accepted it by saying: "We shall do, and we shall hearken." [16]

If this story is somewhat derogatory to the reputation of Israel's neighbors, it is nonetheless quite true to the picture we get from other sources about the state of morality in the ancient world. If, however, we are able to detect in this story just the slightest hint of Israel's ascribing any undue merit to itself, then we find this impression corrected in another part of rabbinic literature. Far from voluntarily rushing into the covenant, and accepting the obligations of the Torah, Israel is there pictured as standing at the foot of Mount Sinai, while God is lifting up the mountain, holding it over the people "like a barrel," and saying to them: "If you accept the Torah,—fine. If not, this will be your grave." [17]

There is something harsh about this particular picture which is worlds apart from the manner in which we today understand a religious commitment. And yet, there is something to be said for the accuracy of that picture, if not as a reflection of the events at Sinai, then, at any rate, as a metaphor for the inexorable nature of Jewish destiny, of the covenant which was

made "with him that standeth here with us this day
before the LORD our God, and also with him that is not
here with us this day." (Deuteronomy 29:14.) As the
Rabbis recognized long ago: "If you are different from
the nations of the world, then you are on God's side.
But if not, then you are left to Nebuchadnezzar and
his like, (—the persecutors)." [18]

The Mystery

Yet when all the interpretations and explanations
of the "election" and the "covenant" have been read
and understood, the fact itself remains what it has always been: a mystery. The modern mind may wish to
shun mysteries, but it would still have to utter in
amazement: "How odd of God to choose the Jews!"
The believing Jew knows that he can never fully pen-
etrate the divine mystery. But he also knows that this
particular mystery is a manifestation of the love of God.
"The LORD did not set His love upon you, nor choose
you, because you were more in number than any
people, . . . but because the LORD loved you. . . ."
Even this "explanation," perhaps the best given thus
far, is, of course, at bottom nothing but a tautology.
Only the effects of the covenant, the results of the
"election" are clear, and a Jewish history of some four
millennia, and the Jewish experience of generation
after generation, testify to them. But the greatest testimony of all is Israel's possession of the Torah. "With

everlasting love hast Thou loved the House of Israel, Thy people; Torah and commandments, statutes and judgments, hast Thou taught us."

Israel was elected *for the purpose of* receiving the Torah. Israel was chosen *for the purpose of* entering into a covenant relationship with the God of the whole world, *in order to* be His "kingdom of priests." Without the Torah, and without the commandments, the "chosen people" ceases to be a meaningful concept, and is liable to degenerate into pagan notions of chauvinism and racism. But, by the same token, if Torah is to mean more to us than the "national literature of the ancient Hebrews" which has curiously survived, it has to be read and understood in terms of the election and of the covenant. The Sovereign of the Universe makes known His Will to man, and, as His instrument, He *chooses* the people of Israel.

Torah and Covenant

Not that the covenant and the Torah are identical. The covenant comes before the Torah, and, before the covenant, the election. First comes the realization that God has acted in a certain manner to bring about the redemption of Israel. Then comes Israel's acceptance of the Rulership of God, its willingness to give Him its undivided loyalty. And only then comes the "giving of the Torah." "God said to Israel: 'I am the LORD thy God, thou shalt have no other gods—I am He whose reign you have taken upon yourselves in Egypt.' And

64

when they had said to Him: 'Yes, yes,' He continued: 'Now, just as you have accepted My reign in love, do now also accept My decrees.' " [19]

But Torah and commandments do come after the covenant. The covenant implies obligations, and, in Judaism, the obligations are spelled out. That is why in the story of the covenant in the days of Joshua, which we have quoted earlier in this chapter, the narrative concludes with the information that "Joshua made a covenant with the people that day, and set them a statute and an ordinance in Shechem." And that is why, in the Pentateuch, the covenant is always the prelude to legislation, and why the speech, in Exodus 19, about Israel's becoming God's "own treasure" is followed by the proclamation of the Ten Commandments. Why this should have been so, and what it can mean to us,— that will be the subject of our next chapter.

CHAPTER FIVE

Giver of the Torah

"PRAISED art Thou, O LORD, Giver of the Torah."
That is how our Torah Blessing ends. The Torah, the
reading of which it introduces, is here ascribed, quite
explicitly and without reservations, to the Authorship
of God. After the election, after the entering into the
covenant, God gave the Torah to His people Israel.

The Bible Speaks

In the Bible we read about the thunder and lightnings at Sinai, about the fire which the people saw, and
about the Voice which they heard. We read that "God
spoke all these words,"—words which were inscribed
on the two stone tables. "And the tables were the work
of God, and the writing was the writing of God." But
not the Ten Commandments alone were given by God.

Throughout the Torah we read time and again: "And the LORD spoke unto Moses, saying, 'Speak unto the children of Israel . . .' " Every piece of legislation, every item of ethical teaching and of historical information, is traced back to this same Source. The whole Torah thus becomes the product of Divine Revelation.

All this, of course, is an attempt to put into human words something which transcends the language of men. When infinite God speaks to finite man, only the language of poetry may try to capture what has transpired. The thunders and lightnings at Sinai, as they appear in the biblical narrative, are an echo sounding through the ages of what had happened there. They testify to the fact of Revelation, to the impact it had on the people. But it is only the man of a prosaic mind, the man lacking in imagination, who would read this biblical account as if it were a news bulletin reporting in every detail what has actually happened.

Each Generation and Its Interpreters

The account, as it stands, would, of necessity, convey different meanings to succeeding generations. The man of the twelfth century may see in it something else than the man of the fourth, while the man of the twentieth century may understand it in yet a different way again. Already a view in the Talmud [1] restricts that which the people heard directly from God to the first two of the Ten Commandments, "I am the LORD thy God," and "Thou shalt have no other gods." The rest was mediated to the people through Moses. And, in turn, this talmudic passage was understood by Maimonides [2] in the sense that the principles of the existence of God and of His Unity (which is what the first two of the Ten Commandments mean to Maimonides) are principles which can be arrived at by means of *reasoning*, for "whatever can be established by proof is known by the prophet in the same way as by any other person; he has no advantage in this respect. These two principles were not known through prophecy alone." That is to say, "hearing the commandments directly from God" means to Maimonides that the ideas which they express are accessible to human reason. But this refers to the first two of the Ten Commandments only. All the other commandments were transmitted to the people by Moses, which—Maimonides explains—means that the people at Sinai heard a sound which was unintelligible to them, but which Moses interpreted for them in terms of the commandments.

Medieval Jewish thought stressed this "sound," or this "voice," which the people perceived at Sinai. To the Jewish thinkers it was inconceivable that God should *speak* to Israel in the same way in which one man *speaks* to another. What Israel heard was not God speaking in human language at all, but a specially "created voice" (*qol nibhra*), or a "shaping of the air into the form of letters which would indicate to the prophet or to the multitude the matters God wanted to let them know." [3] Even the reference to the tables which "were the work of God" (Exodus 32:16) is understood by Maimonides as an indication that the tables were of *natural,* rather than of artificial, origin; "for all natural things are called 'the works of the Lord.' " [4]

The endeavor of the medieval thinkers to look beyond the literal sense of the biblical account remains instructive and suggestive, even though their particular views may no longer be our own. If anything, the "mechanical" view of Revelation, the idea of the finished and completed Book handed down from Heaven, is less acceptable today than it ever was before,—if only, as we have indicated in our first chapter, because nowadays we profess to know something about the literary *history* of which the complete Torah is the end product. We today conceive of Revelation rather as "events occurring in the historical experience of mankind, events which are apprehended by faith as the 'mighty acts' of God, and which therefore engender in the mind of man such reflective knowledge of God as it is given him to possess." [5] The "events" themselves are events which take place in the natural order and in history. It is man's God-given ability to place a certain interpretation on them which is evidence of God's Revelation. God "so chose Israel that He not only led them out of Egypt, but also enabled Moses and the prophets to grasp the significance of that exodus. . . . The Bible is the written witness to that intercourse of mind and event which is the essence of revelation." [6]

Dunkirk and the Red Sea

When, in 1940, most of the British and some of the French forces were evacuated from the French mainland at Dunkirk, there were many who felt that a real "miracle" had happened. The odds against that great rescue work seemed to be so overwhelming. The little steamers and boats from all over England, which were used to augment the resources of the British Navy, hardly seemed adequate to the task expected of them. But the evacuation did succeed, and the German victory, which was so close at that time, was averted. When it was all over, thanksgiving services were held throughout England, and the comparison between Dunkirk and the passing of the Children of Israel through the Red Sea suggested itself to many minds. As a matter of fact, the two events may even be said to have shed light on each other. For just as the event at Dunkirk was a "miraculous" one without any setting aside of the laws of nature, so the event at the Red Sea, invested by later generations with all the elements of a supernatural "miracle," may have been at bottom nothing but a natural occurrence, which was "miraculous" because it happened at the precise moment when Israel was in need of it.

But here the analogy comes to an end. The event at Dunkirk has already been buried in the history books of the Second World War. There does not seem to be any evidence that, in the thinking of the free nations, any great change was wrought on account of what had happened at Dunkirk. No new concept of freedom was born here, no added feelings of responsibility of man for his neighbor. That is why we may still refer to Dunkirk as a "miracle." But nobody has yet been able to claim that Dunkirk was a "Revelation."

Not so the event at the Red Sea, the climax of the

liberation from Egyptian slavery. Here it was God Who "revealed Himself at the sea." [7] Here it was Israel which, there and then, recognized and accepted for themselves the Rulership of God, as they exclaimed, "The LORD shall reign for ever and ever!" (Exodus 15:18.) And this exclamation, this sign of an event apprehended as "revelation," is repeated by the Jew to this day, and always follows the recitation of the *Shema* in the synagogue. It is part of the blessing, already mentioned in our second chapter, which evokes memories of the past redemption, and looks forward to the messianic redemption of the future. But that is not all. The liberation from Egypt, understood as an act of Divine Revelation, necessarily led to the concept of God as the Author of Liberty. And this, in turn, was to lead to a host of provisions in the social legislation of Israel,—provisions motivated by the consideration: "And thou shalt remember that thou wast a servant in the land of Egypt, and the LORD thy God brought thee out thence by a mighty hand and by an outstretched arm." (Deuteronomy 5:15.) Here is the basis for such laws of the Torah as: "The stranger that sojourneth with you shall be unto you as the home-born among you, and thou shalt love him as thyself; for ye were strangers in the land of Egypt." (Leviticus 19:34.)

Love

The event at the Red Sea is but one of many in Israel's history where God is said to have revealed Himself, where God has given man the ability to ex-

perience "that intercourse of mind and event which
is the essence of revelation." Why does God give this
ability to man? Why, at certain moments in the course
of history, does He lift happenings and events from the
level of the routine and the ordinary to that of Revelation? Again, we have to answer these questions in very
much the same way in which we have tried to account
for the Election of Israel: It is because of God's *Love*.
"For God so loved the world . . . ," says the Christian (John 3:16). "With everlasting love hast Thou
loved the House of Israel, Thy people," says the Jew
at the daily evening service; "Torah and commandments, statutes and judgments, hast Thou taught us."
Indeed, as Franz Rosenzweig would have it, the Divine
Love is the *only* content of Revelation. Man, becoming
conscious of this Love of God, hears the divine com-
mand: "Thou shalt love the LORD thy God with all thy
heart, with all thy soul, and with all thy might." Ordi-
narily, of course, love cannot be *commanded*. Only a
lover, in a moment of aroused love, might, and does,
demand of his beloved that she return his love, that she
reciprocate the love shown to her. But that is precisely
what the moment of Revelation does imply. God shows
His Love, and longs for man's love in return. All the
rest is commentary and interpretation.[8]

But as soon as man is able to reciprocate the love, as
soon as man is able to hear the commandment, "Thou
shalt love the LORD thy God," he cannot stop there.
"If I truly love one person," a well-known psycho-
analyst writes, "I love all persons, I love the world, I
love life. If I can say to somebody else, 'I love you,' I

must be able to say, 'I love in you everybody, I love through you the world, I love in you also myself.' " [9] Man, aware of the Love of God, tries to capture, to make concrete and permanent, this experience of Love in terms which will ultimately influence and govern all the affairs of men. And so the experience of God's Love for man results in yet another commandment: "Thou shalt love thy neighbor as thyself,—I am the LORD." (Leviticus 19:18.)

Lest this commandment remain an empty phrase, Judaism spells out in great detail what "loving your neighbor" means; and it spells it out in terms of a host of other laws and commandments. "When man wants to be certain of his existence," the late Dr. Leo Baeck wrote, "when he therefore listens intently for the meaning of his life and life in general, and when he then feels the presence of something lasting, of some reality beneath the surface, then he experiences the mystery: he becomes conscious that he was created, brought into being—conscious of an undetectable, and, at the same time, protective power. . . . And when man looks beyond the present day, when he wishes to give his life direction and lead it toward a goal, when he thus grasps that which defines his life and is clear about it, then he is always confronted with the commandment, the task, that which he is to realize." [10]

The task, the commandment of loving one's neighbor, as Judaism sees it, inspired by an awareness of the mystery of the Divine, involves such things as leaving provisions for "the stranger, the fatherless and the widow" when one is engaged in the act of harvesting,—

and involves it as a matter of *law*, and not merely as a hopeful appeal to the charitable impulses of the moment. (Deuteronomy 24:19-22.) It involves the prohibition of usury, since lending money is understood as help extended to a needy brother. (Deuteronomy 23:20.) It involves a just relation between Capital and Labor. (Deuteronomy 24:14-15.) It even demands that help be extended to one's personal enemy when the latter needs it. (Exodus 23:4-5.) And, needless to say, it rules out any lying and dishonesty, any trickery and corruption. (Leviticus ch. 19.)

All of these, and many, many more are the tasks implied in the commandment that we must love our neighbor as ourselves. And, inasmuch as all this is but a reflection of the Love of God which we have experienced, all these laws may be said to be "divine laws," and "revealed by God,"—even though the thunder and lightnings at Sinai may mean to us no more than an attempt of our ancestors to put into words something that defies adequate description.

Ritual

So far we have been considering one type of Torah law only,—the moral and ethical kind. But, as is well-known, a great part of the legislation of the Torah deals with those acts which are commonly described as "ritual" or "ceremonial." How do they fit into the picture of Revelation? Let us take as our first illustration the laws governing the Passover. The Israelites, as was already mentioned, experienced God as the

"Author of Liberty." Their liberation from Egyptian slavery was understood by them as an expression of God's Will that man must be free. Their own experience of this liberation left an indelible mark on their souls. But how could they transmit this "mark" to their children and children's children? How could they enable future generations to re-live the events of the Exodus? For "re-lived" they must be—both by the complacent Jew, living in freedom, who must be reminded of tasks yet to be accomplished, and by the suffering Jew, in persecution, who must be strengthened in his hope for redemption.

The answer was provided by the detailed provisions of the Passover observance. We eat the kind of unleavened bread they ate. We partake of bitter herbs to remind ourselves of the bitterness of their lives. And we celebrate the *seder* night, thus annually re-living the moment of their liberation. As the Passover Haggadah puts it: "In every generation each Jew must regard himself as though he, too, had been liberated from Egypt." And by regarding ourselves in this light, by celebrating the Passover, we never allow ourselves to forget that the God we worship is the "Author of Liberty," Who wants man to be free. Consequently, all the laws and regulations pertaining to our observance of Passover can be said to be "divine laws."

The Fallacy of Primitivism

In this connection it should be emphasized that, for an observance to be a part of the "divine Law," it

does not mean that the observance cannot have ante-
dated its incorporation into the Torah. For example,
modern scholars are of the opinion that the eating of
unleavened bread was an important part of the spring
festival celebrated by the pagan Canaanite farmers
long before Israel entered Palestine.[11] Yet, what makes
an observance part of the Torah is not at all the meaning and significance which this observance may *originally* have had in a pagan environment, but the meaning *given to it* within the framework of the Torah.
Maimonides already recognized that this was the yardstick to be applied to the whole sacrificial legislation
of the Torah, in which he saw an *adaptation* of pagan
methods of worship to the requirements of Israel's
monotheistic faith.[12] And even Maimonides merely
elaborated a point of view expressed long before him
in the Midrash.[13]

Fascinated as we might well be by archaeological
researches into Hebrew antiquities, we must be on our
guard against committing, what a modern philosopher
of religion has called, the "Fallacy of Primitivism."
This fallacy is committed by the person who is so ob-
sessed with beginnings that he supposes the first stage
of the development of any process to reveal what the
process really is.[14] Guarding against this "Fallacy of
Primitivism," the believing Jew today sees no need to
deny, on dogmatic grounds, that the sabbath may have
originated in Babylonia, or that the dietary laws may
go back to primitive food taboos. What matters to him
is the social and religious meaning given to the *biblical*
sabbath, and the admonition to holiness and self-dis-

cipline which introduces the listing of the *biblical* dietary laws. Such observances, to conclude, are not part of the "divine Law" because they are *"Jewish* inventions," but because they are made to serve a purpose within the Torah's own frame of reference. It is precisely in the hallowing of the ordinary and the customary that the genius of the Torah becomes apparent.

Other Rituals

We have taken the Passover observances as an illustration of the "ritual" or "ceremonial" type of legislation. Though a very familiar illustration, it is, however, not an example of the purely "ritual." The "message" of the Passover does, after all, point to the social and ethical realm. There are, on the other hand, many laws of the Torah which are "ritual" pure and simple, —without any apparent relation to man's moral duties. Here we are thinking of the elaborate sacrificial cult, of the whole realm of levitical purity, and of the many minutiae regulating worship. How could such observances ever have been presented as the "laws of God"?

The answer is not difficult at all. We have seen that Revelation is a manifestation, a *mysterious* manifestation, of the Love of God. It affects levels of man's being far below the conscious one of his rationality,—as indeed all love does. And man wants to hang on to this experience. He wants to re-live it again and again. And, therefore, he tries to create the circumstances which seem to be the most propitious, which seem to have "worked" in the past. In places where God has revealed Himself in the past, it is natural for man to erect temples and sanctuaries,—in the hope of experiencing there future divine manifestations. And it is the love for God, too, which impels a man to elaborate such acts as are understood to be the manner of worshipping Him.

"This is my God, and I will glorify Him," we read in Exodus 15:2. But the Hebrew word, here translated "glorify," really means "beautify." This elicits the question of Rabbi Ishmael: "But is it possible for a man of flesh and blood to beautify his Creator?!" And he answers that the word must be understood as follows: "I shall be beautiful before Him in observing the commandments. I shall prepare before Him a beautiful *lulav,* a beautiful *sukkah,* beautiful fringes, and beautiful phylacteries." [15] On the other hand, Abba Saul, reading the word under discussion (*anvehu*) as *ani vehu* ("I and He"), interprets: "O be like unto Him! Just as He is gracious and merciful, so be thou also gracious and merciful." [16]

Legislation and Commandment

It is interesting to note that here both the "ritual" and the "ethical" are linked to one and the same biblical passage. But this is exactly how the Jew reacts to the Love of God, how he, as it were, returns it on both the "ethical" and the "ritual" level. And, since the

same impulse that is behind the one is also behind the
other, the laws which fence in the two levels are, with
the same logic, traced back to the same Divine Revelation, the same "giving of the Torah." There is, however, as both Buber and Rosenzweig have taught us,
an important distinction which must be drawn between "legislation" and "commandment." Legislation
is "on the books." It has something quite impersonal
about it. Commandment, on the other hand, is that
which is addressed to me *personally*. The legislation of
the Torah is merely the constitution of the ancient
Hebrew commonwealth. Only the Jew who can lift a
given "law" from the level of "legislation" to that of a
"commandment" addressed to him personally, only he
can really re-enact the moment of Revelation, and only
he can experience God as the "Giver of the Torah."
The constant Jewish task, therefore, is that confron-
tation of the Torah which waits for God to utter the
"Thou shalt!"

And what has all this to do with Sinai? The laws and
commandments of the Torah do not all go back to that
moment,—at any rate, not in the form in which we
read them today. They have evolved in the course of
the centuries. Different circumstances called forth different responses. Life in the days of the Hebrew mon-
archy was different from life in the days of the Judges.
And the generations engaged in the task of settling in
Palestine faced different problems from those that be-
set the wanderers in the desert. Yet all the different
responses to all the different challenges were made
from the perspective of the initial commitment at

Sinai, of the "We shall do and we shall hearken" with which the people obligated themselves in the days of Moses. The "giving of the Torah," therefore, is not confined to the occasion at Sinai. It is, as a modern scholar has pointed out,[17] "a concept and a generalization, limited to no single concretization or instance." But it was natural for the biblical writers to link all the legislation, and all the teaching, which, in any case, grew out of the Covenant at Sinai, with that covenant itself.

What parts of the Torah really and truly took on their present form already at Sinai we shall probably never know,—though scholars are still engaged in the discussion of that subject. But for our *religious* orientation, for the *meaning* which Torah can have for us, this hardly matters. However, since our imagination does crave some kind of concrete image, which craving remains unsatisfied by both the poetry of Exodus 19, and the "specially created voice" of the medieval Jewish philosophers, we may well turn to another part of the Bible where the making of a covenant and the acceptance of commandments is described.

A Covenant in the Days of Ezra

There is an account of a "covenant," entered into by the people in the days of Ezra, the circumstances of which we find described in chapters 8 through 10 of the Book of Nehemiah. The assembled people listen to

Ezra's words of exhortation, they join in religious observances, and, as the culmination, we read: "Because
of all this we make a firm covenant and write it, and
our princes, our Levites, and our priests set their seal
to it." (Nehemiah 10:1.)

Then follows a list of the signatories. And then:
"The rest of the people, the priests, the Levites, the
gatekeepers, the singers, the temple servants, and all
who have separated themselves from the peoples of the
lands to the law of God, their wives, their sons, their
daughters, all who have knowledge and understanding,
join with their brethren, their nobles, and enter into a
curse and an oath to walk in God's law which was given
by Moses, the servant of God, and to observe and do
all the commandments of the LORD and His ordinances
and His statutes." (Nehemiah 10:29f.)

After this come individual provisions of the Law.
And this is followed by the statement: "We also lay
upon ourselves commandments." (Nehemiah 10:33.)

There are no thunders and lightnings here, no
mountains trembling, and no earth shaking. There is
just an assembly of the whole people proclaiming: "We
also lay upon ourselves commandments!" But they did
so in response to a soul-stirring religious experience.
It was one of those moments in Jewish history when
God had revealed Himself to Israel.

The covenant in the days of Ezra was, however, only
one of several such covenants which modern scholarship believes to have found in the biblical record. Each
one of the several legal "codes" of the Pentateuch, the

81

existence of which we have mentioned in our first chapter, is said to have been accepted by the people, at various stages of their history, at just such a covenantal assembly. It may not be too farfetched to assume that the pattern of all such covenantal assemblies was set at Sinai, that there are essential features in the covenant described in the Book of Nehemiah which this last of the biblical covenants has in common with the first of these covenants,—the covenant at Sinai. Here, too, after a moment of supreme religious awareness, the Children of Israel constituted themselves as God's "chosen people." And, to carry out that task, they "laid upon themselves commandments," they accepted certain obligations in both the "ethical" and the "ritual" realms. And henceforth, all similar commandments and obligations, which, time and again, the people would lay upon themselves, became part and parcel of that Torah which Israel received at Sinai. The continued process of law-making was but a repercussion of that same Love of God which "chose" Israel and initiated the "covenant."

Admittedly, the description we have attempted above is not the "traditional" one. It is a 20th-century interpretation;—and, as such, it differs no less from the interpretation offered by Maimonides in the 12th century than Maimonides himself differed from his talmudic predecessors. Our interpretation differs from traditional notions in this above all: that the scholarly doubts about the Mosaic authorship of the complete Pentateuch have been taken into consideration. The *fact* of Revelation, and of "the giving of the Torah," is here considered quite independently of any one notion —modern or traditional—about the Torah's literary history.

The "Mosaic Authorship"

Strange as it may seem, however, the *"Mosaic* authorship of the Pentateuch," though generally assumed by Jews throughout the centuries, was not at all what really mattered to Judaism. What was emphasized was the fact that the Torah came from *God!* Rabbinic literature calls him a heretic who asserts: "The whole Torah was dictated by God, but this particular matter was written by Moses of his own accord." [18] One could, in other words, maintain the "Mosaic authorship," and still be called a "heretic." For what mattered here was not really the human agency through which God gave His Torah, but the fact that it was *God* Who gave it. If this was denied, then no belief in the accomplishments of *Moses* could save the concept of Torah. And we have been concerned in this chapter with just this: that behind the literary history of the Pentateuch, behind the various legal codes and narratives, there was the impact of the Love of God, the momentum of a Revelation, which, in a profound sense, enables us to this day to offer our praise unto Him Who is the "Giver of the Torah."

CHAPTER SIX

A Tree of Life

"It is a tree of life to them that grasp it."
(Proverbs 3:18.)

"Said Rabbi Yohanan: 'The greater part of the Torah was given orally, and only the minor part in writing.'"
(B. *Gittin* 60b.)

JUDAISM has never identified the content of Torah with the written text of what the non-Jewish world calls the "Old Testament." The Word of God transcends the merely topical and time-bound. And whenever and wherever attempts are made to capture it within the covers of a book, allowance must be made for the limitations of time and place and of the human scribe. To preserve the flexibility of the Torah, to allow it to keep pace with the moral development of man, and to facilitate the adaptation of its provisions to the ever changing circumstances of life, Rabbinic

Judaism taught the doctrine of the "Oral Torah." Together with the Written Torah which Moses received
at Sinai, so it was said, God gave him the "Oral
Torah," its authoritative exposition, which was never
meant to be committed to writing. It was to have been
passed on, by word of mouth, from master to disciple.
Only the fear, in times of persecution, that "the Torah
would be forgotten in Israel," induced the Rabbis of
the third or sixth centuries of our era to collect in written form the accumulated traditions of the Oral Torah. The result was the Mishnah and the Gemara,
which, together, form the Talmud.

This is not the place to give a full exposition of the
Oral Torah. But a number of considerations must be
adduced here to show that, on the one hand, the belief
in the Sinaitic origin of the Oral Torah probably had
less sweeping implications to those who first pro-
pounded the doctrine than the modern reader might
assume at a first blush, and that, on the other hand, the
position reached by the most recent scientific students
of the Bible could give us a perspective on the Oral
Torah by far more sympathetic than might have been
deemed possible a century ago.

Origin of the Oral Torah

While it is true that the Rabbis of the Talmud ascribed the origin of the Oral Torah to the Mosaic
Revelation, and while there is a statement in rabbinic
literature to the effect that "whatever a disciple of the

wise may propound by way of explaining a law in the most distant future was already revealed to Moses on Mount Sinai,"[1] we would be wrong to ascribe to all the ancient Rabbis the belief that everything now contained in the Talmud and other rabbinic writings does indeed go back, in its present form, to Moses himself. It is true that the idea of religious evolution, or of "progressive revelation," was unknown to the rabbinic Sages. Nevertheless, they were very conscious of the fact that certain provisions of Jewish Law had their origin in the need of meeting certain specific requirements of certain specific times. They actually admitted that some of their Scriptural exegesis was not so much a question of getting the full implications of a text, but rather of using the text as a vague kind of support for a religious provision which they felt the need to enact.

Rabbinic literature contains the legend which describes Moses's being granted a last wish before his death. At his request, Moses was permitted to sit in at a session of Rabbi Akiba's academy (2nd century C.E.). Akiba was expounding the Law in terms so completely unknown to Moses that the latter was stupefied. He regained his composure only when, asked by one of the students for the basis of his remarks, Akiba replied that he was teaching a tradition on the authority of Moses![2]

The sympathies of the modern reader are more likely to be enlisted by the veiled skepticism contained in this last story than by the hyperbolic statement that any innovation in Scripture exegesis likely to be made by a future scholar was already known to Moses himself. Nevertheless, the traditional literature contains a number of statements in support of the antiquity of the Oral Torah which cannot simply be brushed off as unworthy of our serious consideration.

Take, for example, the question of divorce, and of the legal procedure entailed by it. The beginning of the 24th chapter of the Book of Deuteronomy contains the law that a man is not allowed to re-marry his divorced wife after she has been married to a second husband. This restriction is couched in the terminology of biblical case law, and the antecedent clause is worded as follows: "When a man takes a wife, . . . if then she finds no favor in his eyes, . . . and he writes her a bill of divorcement and puts it in her hand and sends her out of his house, . . ." This, be it noted, is the only direct reference to divorce procedure in the Written Law, and, as is abundantly clear, the institution of divorce itself is already taken for granted, and only incidentally referred to. Apologetes for the Oral Torah point out that the Written Torah nowhere tells us what exactly a "bill of divorcement" is, what terminology is to be contained in it, and how the whole procedure of divorce is to be handled. They argue that Moses must have given a full explanation of all the details involved, an explanation which was transmitted by word of mouth as part of the "Oral Torah." If we did not assume this, the scant reference to divorce in Deuteronomy 24 would not make sense.[3]

Again, when we are enjoined, in Leviticus 23:40, to take on the Festival of Sukkoth "the fruit of goodly trees, branches of palm trees, and boughs of leafy trees, and willows of the brook," and when we then find a universal consensus of opinion among Jews that the "fruit of goodly trees" is the *ethrog* (and no other kind of goodly fruit), and that "boughs of leafy trees" refer to the myrtle (and to no other kind of luxurious vegetation), we are, it is argued, forced to assume that Moses provided an oral interpretation that was preserved along with the written text.[4]

No doubt, other explanations besides the Oral Torah hypothesis could be advanced to account for the traditional divorce procedure, and for the choice of specific plants on the Festival of Sukkoth. But in a period like ours, when Bible scholars, particularly those associated with the Scandinavian school, have shifted their attention from the earliest *literary* strata of the Hebrew Bible to the tracing of *oral traditions* which preceded the literary repercussions, it should not be too hard to accept the view that what we have in front of us, black-on-white, in the pages of the Bible, is only a part (perhaps only a minute part) of the totality of biblical tradition which existed in oral form long before any of it was committed to writing. In other words, we can now maintain, on scientific grounds, that much of what is contained in the Hebrew Bible can be fully understood only in the light of the early *oral* traditions of Israel. But this is precisely what is implied by the doctrine of the Oral Torah!

Diversity in Interpretation

Though the Hebrew phrase, *torah shebe'al peh,* which we have rendered as "Oral Torah," is frequently translated as "Oral *Law,*" we have to bear in

mind what has already been pointed out in our first
chapter: that the connotation of the word *Torah* is not
exclusively a legal one. Law is undoubtedly a part of
it, indeed an important part; but it contains much else
besides. This distinction is important, for, while the
teachers of the Oral Torah endeavored with all their
might to achieve unanimity in the interpretation of
the strictly legal passages of the Torah, the greatest lee-
way was allowed in the interpretation of the non-legal
parts of the traditional teaching. It was conceded, for
example, that the words of the Torah lent themselves
to seventy different interpretations. The verse spoken
by Jeremiah in the name of God, "Is not My word like
fire . . . and like a hammer which breaks the rock in
pieces?" (Jeremiah 23:29) was understood as likening
the divine word to the sparks resulting from the hammer's impact upon the rock,—each spark contained
part of the revelation, but no single spark its totality.[5]

It has already been pointed out that the ancient
Rabbis did not share our modern concepts of religious
evolution and "progressive revelation." They were, in
fact, lacking in some of the most elementary notions
of history which today we simply take for granted.
What this implied in practice will be demonstrated
here by a few illustrations.

"An Eye for an Eye"

The modern student of Judaism notes a distinct
moral and religious advance in the Pharisaic-Rabbinic
substitution of monetary compensation for the literal

observance of the law of retaliation in Exodus 21:24, "An eye for an eye, a tooth for a tooth." The Rabbis interpreted this verse to mean that the offender must compensate the victim for the loss of the eye or the tooth, rather than that the offender himself should be punished by having his own eye or tooth knocked out.[6] But the Rabbis would never have admitted that this interpretation highlighted their own moral advance over the rough—though just—provisions of a primitive law. They would not have admitted that their interpretation was an innovation. If the law in Exodus 21:24 is said to demand monetary compensation, then this is what the law has *always* meant—from the very day on which it was committed to writing, as they believed, by Moses himself.

"No Earlier or Later"

In accounting for a number of chronological inconsistencies in the Pentateuch, the Rabbis maintained the principle, "There is no earlier and no later in the Torah."[7] That is to say, it is not the intention of the Torah to teach us the precise chronological sequence of the events described. The Rabbis themselves were blissfully unconcerned with questions of "earlier" and "later" in their understanding of biblical history and of its characters. A charming anachronism is, therefore, an inevitable part of all their descriptions of biblical figures. It was, for example, inconceivable to them that the Patriarchs, Abraham, Isaac, and

Jacob, who lived long before the Sinaitic Revelation, should have found such favor in the sight of God without having followed the dictates of the Torah. That they were pious men is both implied and explicitly stated in the Torah itself. But piety to the Rabbis could only mean piety as expressed in the forms known at the time of the Talmud. Consequently they taught that the Patriarchs observed the Torah even before it was revealed to their descendants at Sinai.[8] (Of course, an element of polemics and apologetics might have been involved in this particular case, since Paul and the early Church Fathers made much of the fact that Abraham was "saved" by "faith," and not by "works.")

This sort of thing can be laughed out of court by a sophisticated invocation of the canons of historical research. But such anachronisms sometimes serve as the vehicle for the transmission of profound spiritual insights. How much true Jewish sentiment, for example, is revealed in the Rabbis' view of King David! The wars which, according to the Bible, David so successfully fought are the "dialectics of Torah study." The armies he is said to have recruited are the bands of scholars and disciples with which he surrounded himself. And David never took a step without first consulting his *beth din,* his Rabbinical court of law.[9] In short, if King David was to merit the love and esteem in which he was held by Israel, if he was in truth to be the ancestor of the Messiah, it was surely not too much to believe that he conducted himself no less "Jewishly" than a recognized Jewish leader at the time of the Rabbis.

But this soft-pedaling of what few military glories there were in early Jewish history is typical of the whole Oral Torah outlook on life. You can detect it in the silence which the Talmud preserves on the whole chain of events leading up to the institution of the Chanukkah Festival. A victory of the Hasmoneans over the "Greeks" is indeed referred to, but only to set the stage for the "miracle of the oil" in a rededicated Temple.[10] Judah the Maccabee is not even mentioned by name!

You find it also in the story of the Rabbi who visited a Palestinian town, and asked to see the "guardians of the city." When shown the local militia, he called them "the destroyers of the city," and pointed to the scholars in their school as the city's true "guardians." [11]

Thus, while some "Old Testament" scholars may tell us that early Israel adopted YHWH as a "war god," the Rabbis, for their part, know of "the Book and the Sword which came down from heaven together," [12] and they also know that Israel opted for the Book. Characteristic of their whole attitude are the early rabbinic comments on the law about the altar of stone found in Exodus 20:25f.: "And if you make Me an altar of stone, you shall not build it of hewn stones; for if you wield your tool (lit. 'sword') upon it you profane it. And you shall not go up by steps to My altar, that your nakedness be not exposed on it."

This is the biblical law. By the time of the Rabbis animal sacrifice was no longer a part of the Jewish manner of worshipping God, and one might have thought that this law was of historical and archaeological interest only. But this is what the masters of the Oral Torah made of it: "The altar is made to prolong the years of man, and iron is made to shorten the years of man. It is not right for that which shortens life to be lifted up against that which prolongs life." Furthermore, "the stones for the altar do not see nor hear nor speak. Yet, because they serve to establish peace between Israel and their Father in Heaven, the Holy One, blessed be He, has said: 'Thou shalt not lift up an iron tool upon them.' How much the more, then, should he who establishes peace between man and his fellow-man, between husband and wife, between city and city, between nation and nation, between family and family, and between government and government, be protected so that no harm should come to him!" And again, "the stones of the altar have no sense of what is proper or improper. Yet God said that you should not treat them disrespectfully. It is, therefore, but logical that you should not treat with disrespect your fellow-man, who is made in the image of Him by Whose Word the world came into being." [13]

Four Methods of Exegesis

What should not be left out of sight, however, is the fact that, in addition to these spiritual implications, the Rabbis also recognized that the law about the altar of stone had a very real and concrete application in the sacrificial service of ancient Israel. This brings us to the question of how the teachers of the Oral Torah looked upon their own work. The Sages of the Talmud established the norm that "no verse of Scripture ever departs from its literal meaning"; [14] that is to say, homiletical interpretations should be clearly taken for what they are, and not be allowed to encroach upon the literal application of the sacred text. Nevertheless, it is not too often that we find the Sages abiding by this norm. The whole development of Rabbinic Judaism (in contrast to the early Sadducees and the later Karaites who maintained a literalist and "fundamentalist" position), necessitated a frequent disregard of the literal meaning of the biblical text. It was only in the 13th century, and then possibly under the influence of the scheme which Christians had earlier adopted for their exegesis, that we find in Jewish sources a clear recognition of the four different methods of exegesis with which the Oral Torah approaches the text of the Written Torah.

There is, first of all, the *peshat,* the literal meaning of the text. Then there is *derash,* the homiletical exposition. Then comes *remez,* the typological and allegorical sense of the text. And finally there is *sod,* which is the sense given to a passage by the mystics.

Naturally, there were many commentators who were striving to get at the *peshat,* at the literal meaning of a text. But the *peshat* turns out to be a very elusive thing. What one generation may regard as the literal meaning of a biblical text may be considered "preaching" pure and simple by a succeeding age. Look, for example, at the Jewish scholars in the Islamic world who followed in the footsteps of R. Saadia Gaon (10th century). Forced by the necessity of meeting Karaite opposition to Rabbinic Scripture interpretation, they could not but base their defense of Rabbinic Judaism on what they considered to be the *peshat* of the Bible text. And yet, looking back upon them from the vantage-point of the 12th century, Abraham Ibn Ezra regarded their commentaries to be about as close to the literal meaning of the text as is the circumference of a circle to its center! [15]

Ibn Ezra, for his part, was insistent that he was interpreting the Bible according to its pure *peshat,*— according to Reason, and in strict conformity to the rules of Hebrew grammar. But Ibn Ezra was likewise a child of his time. Not only was he acquainted with medieval science and philosophy, but he happened to have been a believer in Astrology as well! Thus, while he may be highly critical of all of his predecessors in the field of Bible interpretation for failing to do justice to the plain literal meaning, Ibn Ezra himself will not infrequently astonish the modern reader who is looking for the highly vaunted *peshat* with choice bits of Aristotelian psychology and with astrological notions.

In the case of Rabbi Solomon ben Isaac—better known as Rashi—(11th century), the most popular Bible commentator of all, we see a man who is likewise aiming at the *peshat.* But for him this means more often than not to pick out of a variety of rabbinic homilies on a given text the one which makes the least demands on our credulity, and which is most easily reconciled with the actual wording of the biblical text. Rashi's grandson, however, Rabbi Samuel ben Meir, did make considerable advances in the field of *peshat*. Thus, in his comments on Exodus 13:9 ("And it shall be to you as a sign on your hand and as a memorial between your eyes . . ."), a verse in which Jewish Tradition sees a clear reference to the commandment of phylacteries (*tefillin*), Samuel ben Meir refers to Song of Songs 8:6 ("Set me as a seal upon your heart, as a seal upon your arm . . ."), and clearly states that just as the latter verse has a purely figurative meaning so does the former. This, of course, does not mean that Rashi's grandson dispensed with the observance of putting on phylacteries. He knew that he was bound to observe this commandment as part of the Oral Torah, and he recognized in the Scripture verse a "hint," a mnemotechnical device to which the commandment of phylacteries could be linked. But as for the literal meaning of the verse, he, the representative of *peshat*, had to admit that it merely means: the events described in this biblical chapter, i.e., the Exodus from Egypt, "should be remembered by you always, *as if* they were written upon your hand."

It can perhaps be said that the method of *peshat*, where it is really successful, is that aspect of the Oral Torah which comes closest to the methods of modern critical scholarship. And yet, the question remains whether the real *peshat* can ever be discovered. We saw that Saadia Gaon and his successors, while endeavoring to give the *peshat*, were nevertheless subject to the limitations of their time and their environment. So was Rashi, and so indeed was even a man like Ibn Ezra! It is not different with the modern scholarship of the Bible. Here, too, as we have noted in our first chapter, the "scientific" presuppositions are not a little indebted to current philosophical notions, and, therefore, liable to change with any change in the general philosophical climate. Of course, as long as the search for truth motivates human efforts, the search for *peshat* will always remain a significant aspect of the Jewish approach to the Bible. But it should be clear by now that Judaism, as it has developed over the millennia, is not now, if it ever has been, identical with the literal meaning of the text of the "Old Testament."

That is why the Rabbis recognized the importance of *derash*, the derivation of the text's implicit meaning —as they understood it. Thus, the comments quoted above on the law about the altar of stone would be considered *derash* on the text of which the *peshat* is merely concerned with the prohibition of the use of hewn stone for the erection of an altar. On the other hand, to refer to another illustration we have already mentioned, the interpretation of the biblical law of retaliation in terms of monetary compensation would be considered the actual *peshat* of that text—notwithstanding the quite different *peshat* which ancient Sadducees and modern scholars would find there.

A *derash* interpretation may keep rather close to the wording of the biblical text, but it may also go to extremes. It may account for a grammatical irregularity, such as the mention of stones (in the plural) in Genesis 28:11 and the mention of only a single stone in Genesis 28:18, by telling us that all the stones at Beth-el were vying for the honor of having the Patriarch Jacob use them as a head-rest, so that God united them all into one single stone.[16] But, in addition to perpetuating such folkloristic elements, *derash* interpretation also served as a channel for the transmission of Platonic notions to the Jewish academy. Thus, in a comment on the first verse of the Bible, it is said that the Torah preceded the creation of the world. God is pictured as consulting the Torah in the act of creation just as an architect would consult his blueprints.[17] In fact, any attempt at systematizing Jewish theology is largely dependent on *derash* exegesis for source material,—which, of course, is precisely what we have been doing in this study on the meaning of Torah.

The method of *remez*, of finding an allegorical meaning in the Scriptures, was the method largely followed by the Hellenistic Jews of Alexandria, of whom Philo Judaeus (1st century C.E.) was the outstanding representative. This method became very important for the Christian Church, but it hardly had any impact on the development of the Oral Torah. There is, however, one exception: When it came to the Song of Songs, the Rabbis considered the allegorical interpretation the only legitimate one. Instead of taking literally the references in that book to the young lover and his beloved, the Rabbis maintained that the whole book was an allegory of the love between God and Israel.

Though the allegorical interpretation of the Song of Songs may have little to commend itself to the modern mind, it will have to be conceded that we owe the canonization, and hence the very preservation, of this delightful book solely to this interpretation. Rabbi

Akiba was thinking of the allegorical meaning when he exclaimed that, of all religious poetry, the Song of Songs was the "holy of holies." [18] Later in the development of Jewish thought, the method of *remez* was applied by Maimonides to other parts of the Bible, to the "Wisdom Books" in particular; and, in his skillful hands, it was turned into an instrument of philosophical enlightenment.

The perspective of *sod* (lit. "secret") was that of the mystics, who maintained that every single word of the Torah had a deeper meaning than the obvious sense evident to those not initiated into the mysteries. As the Zohar, the "Bible of Jewish Mysticism," puts it: to the ordinary *bona fide* Jew "we impart the revealed matters of the Torah. That is to say, we make known to him the general outlines, and we caution him about the strict observance of the commandments of the Torah. But no more—unless he rises to another level." And this "more" is understood as "the mysteries of the Torah, and the secrets of the Torah, which one need not reveal except to him who has reached a suitably higher level." [19] Indeed, the very function of the Zohar, that major work of Jewish mysticism which, in its structure, represents a running commentary on the Torah, is to point out these "secret" meanings of the text. It is, moreover, sufficiently obscure in style and language to remain relatively inaccessible to the ordinary reader who comes to it without the requisite preparation. Considering the doctrine of "emanation" and other Neo-Platonic notions which are mediated by the Zohar, it may be said that the method of *sod* provided another opportunity for Philosophy to be assimilated to basic Jewish concepts. On the other hand, it must likewise be admitted that of all the ways of Jewish Scripture exegesis the way of *sod* lent itself best to the most far-reaching aberrations.

The Torah Literature

From all that has been said above it follows that, when the Jew says that he is "studying Torah," he does not mean at all that he is limiting his attention to the Pentateuch, or even to the collection of "Pentateuch, Prophets and Writings," which is called the Hebrew Bible. It means that he is taking the totality of Rabbinic literature for his province. The earliest part of that literature, the Tannaitic Midrashim of the first few centuries of the present era, took the form of running commentaries, mostly of a legal character, on the biblical text. The Mishnah, of the same age, though not actually a running commentary like the Tannaitic Midrashim, is nevertheless based on the Oral Torah's understanding of biblical legislation. The Gemara, which, together with the Mishnah, makes up the Talmud, is in a way a commentary on the Mishnah, while a considerable part of Jewish literature through the ages also took the form of commentaries and super-commentaries on the Talmud.

The various legal codes, of which type of literature the 16th-century *Shulḥan 'Arukh* is perhaps the best-known example, are basically an attempt to present the law of the Torah, as developed by the Talmud, in more accessible compendia, and, in their turn, they gave rise to a host of commentaries and super-commentaries keeping the law "up-to-date." At their side there arose the literature of "Responsa," which, dealing with questions of the concrete application of the Law, again reflected the dynamic and flexible nature of the provisions of the Torah.

That homiletical literature—the early and later collections of Midrash—is by definition nothing but the application of the method of *derash* to the exegesis of the Bible goes without saying. And we have already seen that the Zohar, too, purports to be a "commentary" on the Torah.

What may need stressing, however, is that even the philosophical literature of Judaism is, in the last analysis, a way of interpreting the Torah. It represents an attempt at reconciling current philosophical notions with the doctrines derived from the Bible, or, where that is not possible, at defending the Torah against philosophical attacks. A considerable portion of the *Guide for the Perplexed* by Maimonides is given over to the interpretation of biblical expressions. According to its author's Introduction, "This treatise has as its principal object to clarify the meaning of certain terms in the Bible." And even the works of such moderns as Hermann Cohen and Franz Rosenzweig are to a very large extent concerned with a philosophical exegesis of the Torah.

"Torah," in the words of the late Professor Samuel S. Cohon, "is living and dynamic religion. It is Juda-

ism embodied in our literature and tradition. It con-
stitutes the ideal stream of Jewish religious creativity
and the norms of moral and spiritual living." [20] Every
part of that vast literature of Torah bears the stamp
of its own age and the mark of its inevitable limitations.
But, at the same time, every page of this literature
proclaims that Torah, for the Jew, is the living and
ever-present Word of God, confined to no single book
of ages past, though having its anchor in that covenant
which the God of Israel made with His chosen people.

Here, then, is the clue to the secret of Judaism's
survival, the reason why the literary remnants of an
ancient Mediterranean people can yet merit the epithet
of "a tree of life." Through study and practice, through
a prayerful approach in the words of the psalmist,
"Open Thou mine eyes, that I may behold wondrous
things out of Thy *torah*," (Psalm 119:18) the modern
Jew may yet see in the Torah a guide-post in his search
for the Will of God in the "here and now." For, as
Leo Baeck has said, "Judaism did not affix itself to any
particular period so as to finish up with it; never did it
become complete. The task abides, but not its solution.
The old revelation becomes a new revelation: Judaism
experiences a *continuous renaissance*." [21]

CHAPTER SEVEN

To Study and to Do

O, our Father,
Merciful Father,
Thou Compassionate One, have compassion upon us;
And set it in our heart
To understand and to comprehend,
To hearken, to study and to teach,
To observe, to do and to perform
All the teachings of Thy Torah
In love.

(From the *Ahavah Rabbah* prayer.)

THE preceding pages offer the reader a *theory* of Torah. They attempt to develop a point of view which, though conscious and aware of the findings of modern scholarship, yet bases itself on an inner relationship to the material considered. In terms of our initial metaphor, the form and contents of the "marriage contract" have been studied in the light of the "love letters" which Israel has written, read, and cherished. Neither the compilation of the findings of modern biblical scholarship, nor, again, the writing of a comprehensive history of Torah literature, have been the objectives of this book. Rather have we been concerned with the *meaning* which Torah can have for the modern Jew.

Yet Torah has never been a mere concept to satisfy intellectual curiosity. It has never been a mere matter of belief, or of dogmatic formulation. Torah has been all of these. But it has also been infinitely more. It was about Torah that Rabbi Simeon said: "Not study is the chief thing, but action." [1] The study and the comprehension of Torah must lead to deeds, to a way of life in which Torah finds concrete expression.

The "Orthodox" Approach

It is in the realm of "action" that Torah has become problematical for the modern Jew. Theoretically at least, the problem does not exist for the "Orthodox" Jew. For him, every single word of the Pentateuch represents the very Word of God, without any alloy contributed by the human channels through which it flows. And where the word of the Scriptures, taken literally, militates against either the voice of conscience or against the possibility of fulfilment, he is bound to understand it in the light of the rabbinic commentaries which are likewise traced back to the Sinaitic Revelation of both the Written and the Oral Torah.

Above all, the detailed provisions of the Torah come to him as part of a legal system by which he still con-

siders himself bound. The so-called Five Books of
Moses are both the constitution and the legislation of
ancient Israel. We do not know how widely accepted
they were in the days of the First Temple. The Hebrew Prophets, at any rate, paint a rather gloomy picture. But we do know that, at the beginning of the
Second Jewish Commonwealth, the people solemnly
bound themselves by an oath and a "firm covenant" to
abide by that Law.[2] It was in this solemn oath and
covenant that later generations were to see *the* source
of authority behind the legislation of the Second Jewish Commonwealth. There were disagreements. The
Pharisees and the Sadducees had different understand-
ings about the obligations involved in this covenant.
But those disagreements had reference not to the
source of that authority, but to the scope to which it
extended.[3]

The "constitution" thus adopted by Israel survived
the destruction of the second Jewish state. The Rabbis
of Mishnah and Gemara carried on the administration
of the old law. Allowance was, of course, made for the
changed circumstances. The traditional laws were di-
vided into those that were obligatory in the Holy Land
only, and those to be observed wherever a Jew might
find himself.[4] The civil law of the non-Jewish environment was even declared to be religiously binding upon
the Jew, where it did not conflict with his religious
requirements.[5] But withal there remained a large body
of Jewish legislation, which could all the more be en-
forced because, throughout many centuries, the Jews,
in diverse places, were given a considerable amount of

autonomy. To the divine authority behind Torah Law there was thus joined the legal autonomy enjoyed by the Jewish courts. Even where this tended to disappear in modern times, the closely-knit life of the Jewish communities resulted in the kind of conformity which only those prepared to break completely with their home environment would have dared to ignore.

To this day, the real "Orthodox" communities profit by this environmental factor. Where everybody else observes the Sabbath in a certain manner, he would become an "outsider" who acted differently. Where all meals are being prepared in accordance with the traditional dietary laws, a disregard of the latter becomes the mark of "apostasy."

Religious belief and environmental factors thus combine to enable the traditionalist Jew to live as if the old constitution and legal system were still in force. There may be problems about details. May the gas flame be turned off on a festival day, or not? [6] Or may an automatic elevator, set in motion the day before, be used on the Sabbath day? In other words, there are problems in adjusting the traditional legislation to the technological advances of modern living. But they are problems of *detail*. The *principle* remains unchanged. And the principle is one which maintains the unbroken chain of authority. This authority was divinely bestowed upon Moses, and transmitted by him to Joshua, and by Joshua to the elders, by the elders to the Prophets, and so on, down the line, up to, and including, the latest duly ordained rabbi who is authorized to decide questions of ritual and civil law.

Modern Doubts

The non-orthodox Jew today finds himself in disagreement with the imposing system of Tradition on two counts. In the first place, he has given up the belief in "Verbal Inspiration." He is conscious of the *human* element in religious institutions and observances, and, last not least, in the very documents of Torah themselves. The "mechanical" view of Revelation, which would make of Moses, at best, the faithful stenographer of God, completely unaffected by the factors of human personality, is one which does not commend itself to the modern mind. In addition, of course, there is, as we have already remarked in an earlier chapter, the modern knowledge, or presumed knowledge, about the evolution of ancient Hebrew literature. And this knowledge operates in terms of different institutions and legal provisions, called forth by different and varied social, cultural, and political conditions.

In the second place, the non-orthodox Jew has partly acquired his heterodoxy precisely because, for him, the continuous and autonomous Jewish environment has broken down. In fact, he regards it as having come to an end ever since the time of the American and French Revolutions, when Jews began to step out of the ghettos into the world of Western civilization. Neither the feeling of being subject to rabbinic authority, nor an "other-directedness" based on the norms of conformity in a closed Jewish environment, are applicable motivations in his case.

Basic to the non-orthodox Jew is the *voluntary* nature of religious affiliation in a modern democratic society. He can neither hold beliefs at variance with his own philosophical convictions, nor can he conduct himself as though compelled by ecclesiastical authority. But that such a modern orientation need not conflict with a belief in Revelation as such has, we trust, already been demonstrated in the preceding pages. Nor, as has been shown, does a knowledge of modern biblical criticism preclude the belief that the Word of God is contained in the Scriptures as well as in the Oral Torah.

What, however, is this modern Jew supposed to *do* by way of practising the provisions of the Torah? He could, of course, *voluntarily* subject himself in one "leap of action" (to borrow a phrase of Abraham J. Heschel's) to the full regimen of Orthodox Jewish Law. That is to say, he could silence his own doubts, and terminate the anguish of his own personal search, by finding complete spiritual fulfilment in the traditional modes of Jewish living. He could do so even without becoming "Orthodox" in theory by regarding this step as purely his own personal solution, and by refraining from taking a censorious attitude towards those who are unwilling to take the identical step.

Yet it is unlikely that this step would appeal to the majority of modern Jews,—gratifying as it might well be in the case of individuals. Here we must revert to a point already made in Chapter Five: the distinction between "legislation" and "commandment." "Legislation" is something that is "on the books." A "commandment," on the other hand, is addressed to *me* personally. Now, it may well be that much of the legislation found in the Torah originated as "commandments" experienced by ancient Israel. But it is also true that, in the course of time, it did become "legislation," and, as such, applicable only to the everyday life of a community governed by this legislation.

The modern Jew, as we have defined him, lacks the awareness of living in such a community, and, therefore, also the prerequisite for re-translating the cold letters of legislation into the personally meaningful and significant sounds of commandments. This is not to say that the modern Jew rejects the idea of "community" as such. Even the non-religious Jew in America is often very community-minded. But it just is no longer the kind of community which would accept a 16th-century, or even a 3rd-century, formulation of Jewish Law as its constitutional basis. The large American Jewish community, with its hospitals and its welfare funds, with its Jewish Centers and its "defense agencies," is basically a *secular* community. It may contain the seeds out of which a religious revival might one day sprout. But the religious revival itself has not yet taken place. This much, then, is clear: that the kind of "holy community" which enabled the Jew in the past to experience legislation as commandment is one no longer known to the modern Jew.

Listening for the Commandment

By thus stating the diagnosis we have already hinted at the cure. In the first place, the modern Jew must regain the frame of mind in which he is able to experience the "commandment" addressed to him. It is a frame of mind which the Rabbis of old attempted to create, when they insisted that the Revelation at Sinai must be as topical to the Jew as if it had happened to him "*today.*" [7] It is also a frame of mind to which the modern Jew *can* attain, as has been demonstrated by Franz Rosenzweig, both in his thought and in his way of life.[8]

How does one set about listening for the commandment? There could hardly be a hard-and-fast rule for this. But one of the prerequisites is undoubtedly the willingness and the readiness to shape one's whole life according to the pattern which God gives us to see. And we do not have to start from nothing! The accumulated heritage of the Jewish past is ours to select from, ours to experiment with, in our endeavor to find out what God wants *us* to do.

Consider, for example, the case of the man who, after sober reflection, has come to the conclusion that one of the ways in which he can make God more real in his life is that of self-discipline. He cultivates the habit of saying "No" to himself occasionally. He is now looking for a regimen which would place this kind of self-discipline on a more permanent basis. He might hit upon the idea of abstaining from certain kinds of meat, such as beef or lamb.

Now, if this man were a Jew, a moderately informed kind of Jew, he would find such a system of self-discipline ready-made for him in the pages of the Torah. This he could adopt as a whole, or in part. The meat from which he abstains would then not be lamb, but pork. Moreover, in addition to cultivating self-discipline for his own spiritual welfare, he would, at the same time, strengthen his links with the Jewish past and the Torah tradition. Above all, he would furnish an example of how a cold letter of dietary legislation could become a living "commandment."

It is thus clear that the modern Jew in search of the "commandment" addressed to him must, as a starting-point, engage in intensive Jewish study. A daily period set aside for this task is surely within reach of all. Yet the moment a decision for Jewish study has been reached, an important "commandment" has already been accepted. Of all the things a man can do which, according to the Rabbis, would yield him enjoyment both in this world and in the next, the "study of Torah" ranks as the greatest.[9] For, with all the emphasis which is placed on "action" rather than on "study," the latter is far from being underestimated. The Rabbis recognized that "study leads to action." [10] It will certainly do so in the case of the modern Jew who studies *in order* to discover what to *do*.

And that is why study will have to go hand-in-hand with "experimentation." The modern Jew, fumblingly at first, and overcoming his initial shyness, will want to "try out" those practices and observances which *might* contain God's commandment to *him*. Here, practice is the only way to find out. Only by actually *trying* to observe it, will he be able to discover whether he is dealing with a "commandment," or just with another item of what is still only "legislation" to him.

Of course, all of this will be marked by a high degree of subjectivity. There is in it none of the certainty which Orthodoxy promises its adherents, none of the matter-of-factness of complying with the established legislation of a body politic. One individual's observance of the Sabbath, for example, is unlikely to be identical with that of another individual. The former might consider that to be forbidden "work" which for the latter is an indispensable ingredient of his Sabbath "delight." But this is the price which will have to be paid. For the majority of modern Jews, it will either be this or nothing at all.

It is a state of affairs well described by Franz Rosenzweig, when he said that what we have in common nowadays is the landscape, and no longer the common road on which Jews walked in unity from the close of the Talmud to the dawn of Emancipation. The best we can do today is to work at our individual roads in the common landscape. Perhaps the future will again know of a common road, or, more likely, of a common *system of roads.*[11]

The Common Landscape

There is, however, a limit to too much subjectivity, just as there is the need to preserve the "common landscape." In the first place, it must not be forgotten that the modern Jewish individuals, with all their diversities, will, if they are interested in Torah at all, share a common ground and a common aspiration.

We are, after all, speaking of the kind of modern Jew who is anxious to find his way back to the Torah, and not of him who has made up his mind to run away from it. As long, therefore, as there is a willingness to "observe" at all, variations in the minutiae of observance, far from obliterating the common landscape, might even tend to give it a more interesting appearance.

A second consideration is that the very nature of Torah makes it impossible for the modern Jew to remain an isolated individual. Jewish living is community living. The moral imperatives of the Torah require a social setting for their implementation. Some of the major cultic provisions of the Torah stipulate the presence of a *minyan,* the traditional quorum of ten adults. Maimonides listed among the sinners who would have no share in the World-to-Come the Jew, who, *without committing any transgressions,* kept his Judaism to himself and did not perform the commandments together with his fellow-Jews. [12] A Jewish hermit is almost inconceivable. The nearest approach we have ever had to hermits, the sectarians who shunned Jerusalem and went to live in Qumran by the Dead Sea, lived there in a highly organized *community.* The famous Dead Sea Scrolls were written in that community, one of them bearing the title of *Serekh Hayahad,* i.e., "The Community Rule."

The Torah was given to the *People* of Israel. God's covenant is, as we have seen, with the "chosen *people.*" Israel's task is to be "a kingdom of priests and a holy *people.*" But if the historical identity of the people of Israel, in space and in time, is to remain intact, because without the people there would be no covenant, it follows that, over and above the "commandments" which the modern Jewish individual accepts as his *personal* obligation, there will be others to which he will have to submit as a member of the *People* of Israel.

The Torah Heritage

Tradition speaks about the "Six Hundred and Thirteen Commandments" of the Torah. But Rabbi Simlai, who first mentioned that number of commandments, [13] did not proceed to enumerate them. Later scholars differed among themselves as to how one could arrive at that number. For if one were to count only the commandments of the Written Torah, the figure would be less than 613. If, however, the commandments of the Oral Torah were to be added to the biblical ones, then the number would far exceed 613. A whole branch of medieval Rabbinic literature is, therefore, devoted to the task of "enumerating the commandments." Various authors argued on behalf of their own counts. However, as time went on, the enumeration of Maimonides, in his *Sepher Hamitzvoth* ("The Book of the Commandments"), achieved the greatest popularity; and it is generally the enumeration of Maimonides to which reference is made when, in modern works, there is talk of the "Six Hundred and Thirteen Commandments."

Talk there is indeed of the "Six Hundred and Thirteen Commandments," even though no modern Jew—the most pious included—is observing *all* of the "Six Hundred and Thirteen Commandments." No Jew today (or in the past) *could* observe them all, even if he so desired. A large number of the "Six Hundred and Thirteen Commandments" has application to the Jerusalem Temple and to the sacrifical cult. Others have reference to the levitical purity of the priests, a subject which, in turn, is again related to the Jerusalem Temple cult. Still others apply only to a Jewish king and to Jewish judges. In other words, the "Six Hundred and Thirteen Commandments" (whatever they might be, and whatever enumeration of them we might choose to follow) were never meant to be observed by each and every Jew. Nevertheless, the concept of the "Six Hundred and Thirteen Commandments" has become a slogan in modern Jewish life. It is often asserted that Orthodox Jews observe the "Six Hundred and Thirteen Commandments," and that the non-orthodox Jews do not.

That this could not possibly be true of any Orthodox Jew we have already seen. But it is also not true that the non-orthodox Jew rejects the "Six Hundred and Thirteen Commandments" as a whole. If, for example, such a Jew loves his neighbor, then he is observing one of the "Six Hundred and Thirteen Commandments" (by everybody's method of enumerating them). If he refrains from murder, from adultery, and from theft, he is observing a second, a third, and a fourth of the "Six Hundred and Thirteen Commandments." If he pays his employees in time, if he returns a lost article to its owner, and if he honors his father and his mother, then he is observing a fifth, a sixth, and a seventh. There is no need here to keep count of all of the "Six Hundred and Thirteen Commandments" which a reasonably moral non-orthodox Jew does observe. For the traditional count of those commandments does not confine itself to

EVER SINCE SINAI

the so-called ritual and ceremonial observances. The love of one's neighbor is no less a part of that count than is the practice of not mixing meat and milk dishes.

Thus neither the Orthodox nor the non-orthodox Jew can be described as either totally observing or totally rejecting the "Six Hundred and Thirteen Commandments." Both are *partial* observers. Moreover, while the moral and ethical commandments are certainly not a monopoly of the non-orthodox Jew, it can also not be said that even the most radical Reform Jew has completely divested himself of *all* of the so-called ceremonial observances. (Even he might be caught praying once or twice a year.)

Nineteenth-Century Motivations

It is, however, true that, in matters of ritual and ceremonial observances, Reform Judaism has, historically speaking, opted for less of the traditional heritage than have the Orthodox and Conservative forms of Judaism. In the nineteenth century, Reform Judaism gave up many traditional Jewish observances —because, so it was said then, they were "too Oriental," or because they no longer "spoke to modern man."

This was indeed a break with Jewish Tradition—a tradition which knew only of "commandments," without distinguishing between moral and ritual commandments to the detriment of the latter. The student of Jewish history can understand the reasons which led to this state of affairs. He can, on occasion, even find excuses. Nevertheless, the problems of the twentieth century are of an altogether different kind. We no longer believe that the European Jew becomes a better European, and the American Jew a better American, by shedding his Jewish particularism and by assimilating the forms of Jewish piety to those of Christianity.

Moreover, in view of what we know today of psychology, we also have become somewhat more circumspect in our evaluation of "ritual" and of the "non-rational." If it was the task of Judaism in the nineteenth century to "adapt" itself to the "views and habits of modern civilization" (third "plank" of the Pittsburgh Platform of 1885), we, today, are somewhat more critical of that "modern civilization." We rather regard it as the need of the hour to make the nominal Jew into a real Jew. If the nineteenth century felt it to be necessary to tell the Jew what he no longer had to observe, the changes which the twentieth century has wrought call for both the Jew's renewed and intensified acquaintance with his own heritage, and for a set of criteria which he can apply to that heritage, so that intelligent choices may be made from it.

It is, then, with a view to having the modern Jew's study of the Tradition lead to his "doing" that the following criteria are suggested.

The Thrust of Tradition

(1) *What, in any given case, has been the main direction of the millennial Tradition?* In the process of examining the traditional material, one must not

remain satified with first impressions. Rather should one pursue the meaning of a given observance in the Jewish past. Moreover, since, within a span of some three thousand years, the meaning was not always uniformly understood and interpreted, it becomes particularly important to discover the main thrust within the Tradition.

For example, a modern Jew might well be under the impression that the prohibition of work on the Sabbath was simply directed against strenuous physical labor. The weekly day of rest in Judaism, therefore, would be understood in terms of the weekly day of rest, Sunday, in modern Christian and secular society. However, a little more thorough study of Jewish sources will soon lead to the recognition that far more is involved here than the mere abstention from exhausting physical labor. The Jewish Sabbath is the day on which man— who creates and works throughout the week—shows himself to be a *creature*. God alone is recognized as the Creator. And this recognition finds expression in the fact that, on the Sabbath, the Jew refrains from acting as a "creator" and from interfering "creatively" in the normal course of nature. Such interference need not even be thought of in terms of physical exertion. The intent of man to impose his will on nature suffices to break the spell of the Sabbath mood.

But if it is the purpose of the Sabbath to express the thought that God, and not man, is the real Creator, then it follows that the abstention from work, commanded in the Torah, is aiming at something over and above man's relaxation and physical recuperation. Conse-quently, it is not sufficient to argue, as some modern

Jews might be tempted to do: "Cooking and baking were hard work in biblical antiquity. But we today do not have to exert ourselves to do so. That's why it should be allowed for us on the Sabbath!" An argument of this kind is far too superficial an interpretation of both the biblical and the Rabbinic Sabbath regulations.

Needless to say, the Sabbath law (with all of its positive commandments and its prohibitions) contains and implies far more than what we have been able to hint at in connection with prohibition of work. We merely wanted to furnish an illustration of what we mean when we suggest, as *one* of the critera for a modern Jewish observance, that, in any given case, an investigation be made into the main thrust of the millennial Jewish Tradition.

The "Here and Now"

(2) The second criterion could be formulated as follows: *In what manner can I best realize the traditional teaching in my life and in the situation in which I find myself?*

If the first criterion was a purely scholarly and objective one, then this second criterion already contains a conscious application of the principle of personal choice. The *conscious* application of this principle distinguishes the Conservative and the Reform Jew from his Orthodox brother. Orthodox Judaism, for example, is, basically and objectively, quite correct in deducing the prohibition of the use of cars and of electricity on the Sabbath from the biblical prohibition of work—with "work" defined according to the Rabbinic categories. Tradition may indeed be so construed.

But the non-orthodox Jew must also ask himself: "Do I observe the Sabbath better if, on account of the distances involved, I refrain from going to the synagogue on the Sabbath or from visiting friends and the sick? Or is it not just the use of my car which helps me in my observance of the Sabbath, in my particular situation? Does the true observance of the Sabbath compel me to keep my home cold and dark? Or is it not just the use of electricity which helps me to make the Sabbath the 'day of light and joy' it was meant to be?"

In other words, the non-orthodox Jew is far more concerned with the Sabbath itself than he is with the letter of the Sabbath legislation, a letter which testifies to the reality of the Sabbath as experienced by *past* generations in *their* life and in *their* situation. He wants to observe the Sabbath in the "here and now." That is why factors come into play with which the legalists of earlier generations did not have to reckon.

The Voice of Conscience

(3) A third criterion is *the voice of my own conscience.* In this criterion, even more than in the second one, we see the influence, positively affirmed and welcomed, of the Emancipation and of the pluralism which flourishes in the modern secular state. The individual is no longer subject to religious compulsion or to the dictates of any ecclesiastical

authority. As an individual, he is free to participate, and free not to participate—even if others believe that they have found the key to the proper observance of a given commandment in the "here and now." Deducing things from Torah law, even bearing in mind the needs of our particular situation, is not yet the whole story. Conscience still has to assent!

Take, for example, the commandment which states, in connection with Passover, "And there shall be no leaven seen with thee in all thy borders seven days" (Deuteronomy 16:4). There can be no doubt about the main thrust of the Tradition with regard to this commandment. Anything remotely subject to the suspicion that it might contain "leaven" must not only not be "seen" in the Jew's home during Passover. It must not even be in his possession. The application of this understanding of the commandment, as interpreted by the Rabbis, could thus lead to the wholesale destruction of food in the Jew's house just before Passover—were it not for the fact that the same Rabbis who elaborated the stringencies of that commandment also evolved a legal fiction by means of which the full force of the law could be evaded. By "selling" the food to a non-Jew—with a minimum down-payment, and with the understanding that the Jew can buy it all back after the festival—the food need not only not be destroyed, but it can remain on the Jew's premises, provided it be suitably locked up. [14]

There is nothing wrong with legal fictions as such. No legal system can function without them. Indeed, one might even appreciate the inventiveness of the ancient Rabbis which helped them keep their legal system within humane dimensions. But it is one thing to appreciate the phenomenon historically. It is quite another to accept it for oneself—particularly if one feels that legal fictions are more appropriate to systems of civil law than to man's relationship with God.

Thus, while it would be quite possible for the non-orthodox Jew to solve his "leaven problem" along the lines indicated by the Rabbis, possible even within his "here and now," it is conceivable that such a Jew might say: "Yes, it is *possible* to do it this way; *but my conscience speaks against it*. I shall indeed refrain from eating leaven during Passover. I shall even keep all leaven out of sight in my home. But I feel no need for the legal fiction of 'selling' my leaven. This would add nothing to my Passover observance. On the contrary, I would not feel quite intellectually honest were I to make use of that legal fiction. My conscience rebels against it."

In terms of the criterion we have outlined here, the non-orthodox Jew would be justified in using such an argument. But he would also have to add the following: "My fellow Jew, however, also has the right to listen to the voice of *his* conscience—even if his conscience tells him to 'sell' his leaven for the duration of Passover."

The legal fiction of 'selling the leaven' is, of course, only one illustration. There are other provisions in traditional Jewish law which many modern Jews may find impossible to reconcile with the moral sensitivity and the intellectual honesty which themselves are a result of being attuned to the commandments of the Torah.

Responsiblility Toward the
Covenant Community

(4) While the last-named criterion may well carry within itself the seeds of total religious anarchy, the fourth criterion helps to maintain the balance. It is *the feeling of responsibility toward the Covenant Community.*

After all, Judaism cannot be abstracted from the faith-community within which Judaism is lived—the faith-community with which God made a covenant at Sinai, and which remained loyal to Him throughout the millennia. This Covenant People, Israel, not only has a historical significance; its significance extends to the realm of redemptive history. Everything, therefore, which contributes to the survival and to the unity of the Covenant Community of Israel will have to be regarded as a religious "commandment." Everything, on the other hand, which hurts the Covenant Community must be avoided.

Bearing this perspective in mind, the non-orthodox Jew will feel called upon to observe many a "commandment" to which he might otherwise feel no *personal* obligation at all—if, that is to say, his religion were a matter of the individual only, and not also of the community as a whole. Into this category belong the laws governing Jewish marriage and divorce, and the legislation concerning the admission of proselytes to the Covenant Community of Israel. Into this category, too, belong the specific seventh day on which the Jewish Sabbath is to be kept, and all the Jewish festivals, which have to be observed exactly according to the Jewish calendar.

Theoretically, it is conceivable that one might be able to celebrate the ideal of Freedom on some evening other than the Eve of the Fifteenth of Nisan. Americans as a whole do so annually on the Fourth of July. But the *seder,* as a *Jewish* celebration of Freedom, can only be celebrated when the worldwide faith-community of Israel does so; and that is on the Eve of the Fifteenth of Nisan.

In this connection we must also mention the use of Hebrew in the Jewish worship service. Important as it may be to find room for the vernacular in the synagogue, it is nevertheless true that the worshiping Community of Israel knows itself as such particularly during moments of Hebrew prayer.

The Dynamics of Tension

It will not often occur that the four criteria, which we have mentioned, will be in complete accord, all pointing in the same direction. They are more liable to be in a constant state of tension, and different Jews will ascribe different weights to each of the four critera. Yet it is just that tension which represents the dynamic element of Judaism, and the guarantee for its remaining a living faith and a living practice. The four criteria, in their aggregate, represent the yardstick which the modern Jew applies to the inherited Torah Tradition. Yet a yardstick is only—a yardstick. It cannot be the total content of one's religious faith and life. The latter requires more than a yardstick. It needs the material itself, the material of the millennial Torah Tradition. Two thousand years ago, when that Tradition was still relatively young, Hillel stated that "the ignorant person cannot be truly religious." [15] If it was true then, it is all the more true today. Only an intensified Jewish education—of child, youth, and adult—can make the application of the criteria meaningful. But only an application of the criteria can make the Torah Tradition live for us today.

The Individual and the Covenant Community

It is obvious that the subjectivism potentially contained in some of the criteria we have discussed will be checked by the over-all requirements of the Covenant Community. But it is no less obvious that the Covenant Community itself, in its modern form, will become possible only because of the personal commitments of Jewish *individuals*. They are the individuals who have learned to "observe" God's commandments *to them*. In this interplay of spiritual forces, of aspirations and of loyalties, there might well lie the hope of translating Torah from the realm of mere theory into one of "observing, doing, and performing."

Notes

Notes

Notes to Chapter One

1) Cf., e.g., *Midrash Tanhuma, Bemidbar,* paragraph 5.
2) *Tosaphoth* to b. *Menahoth* 20b, s.v. *niphsal.*
3) *Tanhuma,* ed. Buber, *Bereshith,* par. 11.
4) *Mekilta, Bahodesh,* chapter V, ed. Lauterbach, Vol. II, pp. 229f.
5) Samuel Holdheim, *Die Religionsprincipien des reformirten Judenthums.* Berlin 1847, pp. 13f.
6) *Baraitha de Rabbi Ishmael,* in *Introduction to Sifra.*
7) *Genesis Rabbah* 12:15.
8) Edward Robertson: "Law and Religion Amongst the Samaritans," in *Judaism and Christianity,* Vol. III, *Law and Religion,* ed. E. I. J. Rosenthal. London, 1938, pp. 69-72.

Notes to Chapter Two

1) b. *Berakhoth* 16b.
2) Robert Gordis, *Judaism for the Modern Age.* New York 1955, pp. 195-203.
3) Cf. Hayyim Schauss, *The Jewish Festivals.* Cincinnati, U.A.H.C., 1938, pp. 196-199.
4) b. *Berakhoth* 11b; included in the daily morning service.

Notes to Chapter Three

1) *Kuzari* IV, 16.
2) *Kuzari* I, 25.
3) *Kuzari* I, 83ff.

Notes to Chapter Three (continued)

4) Cf. *Mishnah Aboth* 3:7.
5) Cf. *Jeremiah* 28:8.
6) Martin Buber, *Moses*. Oxford, East & West Library, 1947, pp. 52f.
7) b. *Berakhoth* 9b.

Notes to Chapter Four

1) Leo Baeck, *The Essence of Judaism*. London, Macmillan, 1936, p. 55.
2) b. *Berakhoth* 6a.
3) Theodore H. Robinson, *A History of Israel*. Oxford University Press, 1932, p. 92.
4) Cf. Julian Morgenstern: "The Oldest Document of the Hexateuch," in *Hebrew Union College Annual*, Vol. IV, 1927.
5) *Seder Eliyahu Zutah*, ch. 19, ed. Friedmann, Supplement p. 26.
6) Hermann Cohen, *Die Religion der Vernunft aus den Quellen des Judentums*. Leipzig 1919, p. 174.
7) b. *Shabbath* 89a, and cf. Jacob Reischer's commentary *'Iyyun Ya'aqobh* on *'En Ya'aqobh* ad loc.
8) Franz Rosenzweig, *Briefe*. Berlin, Schocken, 1935, p. 376.
9) Sigmund Freud, *Moses and Monotheism*. New York, Vintage Books, 1955, pp. 116f. Italics are my own.
10) Eugene Kohn, *Religion and Humanity*. New York, The Reconstructionist Press, 1953, p. 87.
11) *Genesis Rabbah* 34:7, and parallels.
12) Cf. Alexander Altmann: "Judaism and World Philosophy," in *The Jews—Their History, Culture, and Religion*, ed. Louis Finkelstein. Philadelphia, J.P.S., 1949, Vol. II, p. 657.
13) *Sifré, Vezoth ha-Berakhah*, par. 357, ed. Friedmann, p. 150a.
14) *Numbers Rabbah* 1:6.
15) *Exodus Rabbah* 5:9.
16) *Sifré, Vezoth ha-Berakhah*, par. 343, ed. Friedmann, p. 142b.
17) b. *Shabbath* 88a.
18) *Sifra, Qedoshim*, chapter 11, par. 22, ed. Weiss, p. 93d.
19) *Mekilta, Bahodesh*, ch. VI, ed. Lauterbach, Vol. II, p. 238.

Notes to Chapter Five

1) b. *Makkoth* 24a.
2) *Moreh Nebhukhim* II, 33; and cf. *Malbim*'s commentary on Exodus 20:2.

3) Cf. Judah Halevi, *Kuzari* I, 89, and Maimonides, *Moreh Nebhukhim* I, 65.
4) *Moreh Nebhukhim* I, 66.
5) John Baillie, *The Idea of Revelation in Recent Thought.* New York, Columbia University Press, 1956, p. 62.
6) John Baillie, op. cit., p. 110.
7) *Mekilta, Shirata,* ch. IV, ed. Lauterbach, Vol. II, p. 31, and parallels.
8) Franz Rosenzweig, *Der Stern der Erlösung.* 2nd ed. Frankfort 1930, Part II, pp. 88-151.
9) Erich Fromm, *The Art of Loving.* New York, Harper & Bros., 1956, p. 46.
10) Leo Baeck: "Mystery and Commandment," in *Judaism and Christianity.* Philadelphia, J.P.S., 1958, pp. 171f.
11) Cf. W. O. E. Oesterley and Theodore H. Robinson, *Hebrew Religion, Its Origin and Development.* 2nd ed. London, S.P.C.K., 1937, p. 180.
12) *Moreh Nebhukhim* III, 32.
13) *Leviticus Rabbah* 22:8,—statement by R. Levi.
14) Edgar S. Brightman, *A Philosophy of Religion.* New York, Prentice-Hall, 1940, pp. 37f.
15) *Mekilta, Shirata,* ch. III, ed. Lauterbach, Vol. II, p. 25.
16) Ibid.
17) Max Kadushin, *The Rabbinic Mind.* New York, J.T.S., 1952, pp. 57f.
18) *Sifré, Shelaḥ Lekha,* par. 112, ed. Friedmann, p. 33a; and cf. b. *Sanhedrin* 99a.

Notes to Chapter Six

1) j. *Pe-ah* II, 6, ed. Krotoshin, p. 17a.
2) b. *Menaḥoth* 29b.
3) Cf. D. W. Amram, *The Jewish Law of Divorce.* Philadelphia 1896, p. 12.
4) Cf. David Nieto, *Matteh Dan* II, 120. (Jerusalem ed. 1958, pp. 41f.)
5) b. *Sanhedrin* 34a.
6) b. *Baba Kamma* 83b-84a.
7) b. *Pesaḥim* 6b, and parallels.
8) Cf. b. *Yoma* 28b.
9) b. *Berakhoth* 4a.
10) b. *Shabbath* 21b.
11) j. *Ḥagigah* I, 7, ed. Krotoshin, p. 76c.

Notes to Chapter Six (continued)

12) *Sifré, 'Eqebh*, par. 40, ed. Friedmann, p. 79a.
13) *Mekilta, Baḥodesh*, ch. XI, ed. Lauterbach, Vol. II, pp. 290f.
14) b. *Shabbath* 63a.
15) Ibn Ezra's Introduction to his Commentary on the Pentateuch.
16) Cf. Rashi's commentary on Genesis 28:11.
17) *Genesis Rabbah* 1:2.
18) *Mishnah Yadayim* 3:5.
19) *Zohar, Aharé Moth*, p. 73a.
20) Samuel S. Cohon, *What We Jews Believe*. Cincinnati, U.A.H.C., 1931, p. 117.
21) Leo Baeck, *The Essence of Judaism*. London, Macmillan, 1936, p. 22.

Notes to Chapter Seven

1) *Mishnah Aboth* 1:17.
2) See Nehemiah, chapters 8 through 10, and our discussion of this event in Chapter Five, above.
3) Cf. Jacob Z. Lauterbach, *Rabbinic Essays*. Cincinnati, HUC Press, 1951, pp. 27ff.
4) Cf. *Mishnah Kiddushin* 1:9, and *Sifré Re-éh*, par. 59, ed. Friedmann, p. 87a.
5) Cf. b. *Gittin* 10b and parallels.
6) See the learned article on this subject by Samuel Weingarten, in *Sinai*, Vol. XXII, No. 11 (July 1959), pp. 212-219.
7) Cf. *Sifré Wa-ethhannan*, par. 33, ed. Friedmann, p. 74a.
8) Cf. Nahum N. Glatzer, *Franz Rosenzweig—His Life and Thought*. Philadelphia, Jewish Publication Society, 1953.
9) *Mishnah Pe-ah* 1:1.
10) Cf. b. *Megillah* 26a.
11) Franz Rosenzweig, *Briefe*. Berlin, Schocken, 1935, pp. 426f.
12) Moses Maimonides, *Mishneh Torah, Hilkhoth Teshubhah* 3:11.
13) B. *Makkoth* 23b.
14) Cf. Solomon Ganzfried, *Code of Jewish Law*. Translated by Hyman E. Goldin. New York, Hebrew Publishing Co., 1927, Vol. III, pp.34 - 39.
15) *Mishnah Aboth* 2:5.

Index of Biblical Passages

A Note on
the Rabbinic Sources

A BRIEF survey of the types of post-Biblical literature has been given in Chapter Six. Here we shall confine ourselves to a description of the sources quoted. For further information the reader is referred to Hermann L. Strack, *Introduction to the Talmud and Midrash*. New York, Meridian Books, 1959.

The *Mishnah*, here quoted by "tractates," is the compilation of the Oral Torah, undertaken by Rabbi Judah the Prince around the year 200 of the Common Era. It is still a matter of scholarly debate whether R. Judah merely compiled the material, or whether he also committed it to writing.

The teachers mentioned in the *Mishnah* are known as the "Tannaim." The "Age of the Tannaim" roughly corresponds to the first three centuries of the Common Era.

The Tannaim are also represented in the so-called "Tannaitic *Midrashim*," running commentaries on the legal books of the Pentateuch. There is the *Mekilta* on Exodus, the *Sifra* on Leviticus, and the *Sifré* on Numbers and Deuteronomy.

The teachers after the age of the Tannaim are known as Amoraim. They are represented by the *Talmud*. The *Talmud* consists of the *Mishnah* and the discussions of the Amoraim based on the *Mishnah*. The record of the discussions is called *Gemara*. There are two *Talmudim:* the Palestinian (or Jerusalem) *Talmud*, and the Babylonian *Talmud*. The former was compiled at the beginning of the 5th century, the latter around the year 500. We quote the *Talmud* by "tractates." The letter "j" in front of the name indicates the Palestinian *Talmud*, while "b" indicates the Babylonian *Talmud*.

The *'En Ya'aqobh* is a compilation of all of the non-legal material of the Babylonian *Talmud*, made by Jacob ben Solomon Ibn Habib, a Spanish scholar who died at the beginning of the 16th century.

Tosaphoth is the name given to commentaries and super-commentaries on the Babylonian *Talmud*, written by French and German scholars of the 12th and 13th centuries.

Midrash Rabbah is a collection of expositions and homilies based on the Five Books of Moses, and on the Five Scrolls. The material comes from various times. *Genesis Rabbah* is one of the earliest collections, and is thought to have been compiled about the time of the compilation of the Palestinian *Talmud*. *Leviticus Rabbah*, too, is one of the earlier collections.

The *Tanhuma* is another collection of homilies based on the Pentateuch. It is available in two different editions. The so-called "printed" edition is a medieval collection. The edition by Solomon Buber is held to represent earlier material, going back to the 5th century.

Seder Eliyahu Zutah, one of the so-called "ethical *midrashim,*" is said to have been composed, at least in its present form, in the 10th century.

Index of Rabbinic Sources

Suggestions for Further Reading

THE point of view expressed in the preceding pages has been developed, and more fully documented, by the author in the following articles:—

"The Bible of the Synagogue," in *Commentary*, February 1959, pp. 142-50.

"The Concept of Revelation in Reform Judaism," in *CCAR Yearbook*, Vol. LXIX (1959), pp. 212-39.

"The Dialectics of Reason and Revelation," in Arnold J. Wolf (ed.), *Rediscovering Judaism*. Chicago, Quadrangle Books, 1965, pp. 29-50.

"The Limits of Liberal Judaism," in *Judaism*, Spring 1965, pp. 146-58.

"Not by Bread Alone," in *Judaism*, Summer 1958, pp. 229-34.

"Problems of Reform Halakhah," in *Judaism*, Fall 1955, pp. 339-51.

"Reflections on Revelation," in *CCAR Journal*, June 1966, pp. 4-11.

"Revelation and the Modern Jew," in *The Journal of Religion*, January 1961, pp. 28-37.

"The Supposed Dogma of the Mosaic Authorship of the Pentateuch," in *The Hibbert Journal*, Vol. LVII. No. 227 (July 1959), pp. 356-60.

"Toward a Modern 'Brotherhood'," in *The Reconstructionist*, December 10, 1960, pp. 11-20.

"Toward Jewish Religious Unity," in *Judaism*, Spring 1966, pp. 139-144.

Other statements, and attempted solutions, of the problems dealt with in this book will be found in the following works:—

Jacob B. Agus, *Guideposts in Modern Judaism*. New York, Bloch, 1954, pp. 271-306.

Leo Baeck, *God and Man in Judaism*. New York. U.A.H.C., 1958, pp. 9-23.

John Baillie, *The Idea of Revelation in Recent Thought*. New York, Columbia University Press, 1956.

Bernard J. Bamberger, *The Bible—A Modern Jewish Approach*. New York, B'nai B'rith Hillel Foundations, 1955.

Solomon B. Freehof, *Preface to Scripture*. Cincinnati, U.A.H.C., 1950, pp. 3-78.

Robert Gordis, *Judaism for the Modern Age*. New York, Farrar, Straus, and Cudahy, 1955, pp. 153-85.

Will Herberg, *Judaism and Modern Man*. Philadelphia, J.P.S., 1951, pp. 243-61.

Abraham J. Heschel, *God in Search of Man*. Philadelphia, J.P.S., 1956, pp. 257-78.

Abraham J. Heschel, *Theology of Ancient Judaism*. (Hebrew) London and New York, The Soncino Press, 1962/65, 2 vols.

Louis Jacobs, *Principles of the Jewish Faith*. New York, Basic Books, 1964, pp. 216-319.

Louis Jacobs, *We Have Reason to Believe*. London, Vallentine, Mitchell, 1957, pp. 58-107.

Jacob Neusner, *Fellowship in Judaism*. London, Vallentine, Mitchell 1963.

Jacob Neusner, *History and Torah*. London, Vallentine, Mitchell, 1965.

H. Richard Niebuhr, *The Meaning of Revelation*. New York, Macmillan, 1941.

Franz Rosenzweig, *On Jewish Learning* (ed. N. N. Glatzer). New York, Schocken, 1955, pp. 72-124.

General Index

GENERAL INDEX